Grampian Cookbook

The author

Gladys Menhinick spent her working life in print and publishing. Childhood illness left her with damaged hearing, which is now severe. She has been involved, on a voluntary basis, with issues affecting the hearing-impaired for twenty-five years, including twelve years as chairman of the Aberdeen Association for the Hard of Hearing. As the cookspot presenter on the ITV series *Sign Hear* and *Breakthrough,* her hobbies of cooking and involvement with deaf issues came happily together.

Grampian
COOKBOOK

Gladys Menhinick

MERCAT PRESS
EDINBURGH

First published 1984 by Aberdeen University Press
Second edition published 1993 by Mercat Press,
James Thin, 53 South Bridge, Edinburgh EH1 1YS
Revised edition published 1997

ISBN 1873644 221

For John and Isobel

Printed and bound in Great Britain by
BPC-AUP Aberdeen Ltd.

Contents

Introduction

Grampian Cookbook contains many of the well-loved homely recipes of the North East of Scotland. Some old recipes have been updated to a more modern presentation, or scaled down to suit the smaller household.

The North East produces superb foods — meat, game, fish, cheeses, soft fruit, stone fruit such as plums, and preserves. The distilleries provide a wealth of distinctive malt whiskies, and the water of the ancient and revered spring at the Pannanich Wells near Ballater is now being commercially bottled to bring Grampian a fine mineral water which this year has won a Grampian Good Food Award. The town of Ballater was built to accommodate those who came to sample the spa water of Pannanich, and recent clinical trials at Aberdeen Royal Infirmary have endorsed its health-giving properties, especially in relieving the pain of arthritis.

Despite this choice and the ready availability of good ingredients, it is curiously difficult, when eating out at an everyday level, to find real Scottish food on the menu. Why is there so much of the anonymous, nationless sausage-egg-and-chips type of meal? The all-day-breakfast syndrome of food tasting the same no matter where you eat it? Occasionally, we drive out to eat lunch at a favourite country pub where the cook serves up a piping-hot pot-roast Scotch brisket and gravy, with skirlie and tender root vegetables — a wholesome treat at modest cost. Honest Scottish food cooked and presented in a way much liked in this corner of the country.

A wartime childhood and the lingering shortages of foodstuffs in the immediate post-war years let me see in my own home how tasty meals could be made from just a few rationed ingredients. One of my favourite meals was the stovies my mother made on Mondays. A good knob of dripping went in to melt in the pot (nobody carried on about cholesterol in those days), followed by a pile of chopped onions and tatties from our garden, the little meat scraps and gravy from our small weekend joint, and a tablespoon of water. The lid went on tight and the pot was left 'on a peep' for an hour or so. The stovies were dished up with crispy brown scrapings from the bottom of the pot, and a thin curly bannock to eat with it. Homely and good to eat.

For me, simplicity of approach in cooking is everything — to take just a few ingredients, as fresh and perfect as can be found, and cook them to a simple method that preserves their natural flavours.

In the eighties, cookery competitions caught my interest, the prizes mostly holidays and/or quality kitchen equipment, china and glass. They were fun and for me they were without pressure because of the strictly amateur status of the competing cooks. If I made it through the regional semi-finals, I enjoyed travelling to compete in the final cook-off. Sometimes things went wrong. My sweet at one event was the Blaeberry Puffs (page 40), and I beat the cream so hard it curdled and collapsed, ruined. I learnt from this mistake to take reserve supplies, but I still had a good time.

The highlight was winning a national competition with the Sunshine Meat Roll (page 33), and receiving my prize — a holiday in the Greek Islands — from the actor Ian Ogilvie (*The Saint*). He was a friendly guy and enthusiastic about food. Predictably, I suppose, I found the Greek holiday a glorious adventure into the new-found delights of Greek food, and was particularly intrigued by how local bakers use thyme honey in making cakes and pastries. I came home with some fine recipes.

An invitation from Grampian TV to demonstrate some recipes led to cookspots in the *Sign Hear* and *Breakthrough* series. It seemed a good idea to gather together some of my favourite recipes, and I hope you will enjoy trying some Grampian fare.

Gladys Menhinick
September 1997

 Quantities in the recipes are for four people unless otherwise stated.

 Spoon measures are level.

 Weights are given in Imperial measure, and occasionally in cups and spoons.

As many commodities, particularly meat, fruit and vegetables are still sold in Imperial measures, I have used these familiar measures in the recipes, but have included centigrade temperatures for ovens as these are common now. For conversion purposes 1 oz is approximately equivalent to 25g.

Please note There are health risks associated with raw eggs, which are used as an ingredient in some of the recipes in this book. The publishers and author are not responsible for any ill effects which may result from the consumption of such dishes.

Soups

MOST PEOPLE enjoy a plate of hot soup. Many soups of the Northeast contain meat, or even fish, hearty one-pot soup stews. With a piece of crusty bread and perhaps a little bit of cheese, these soups are complete and balanced meals in themselves. There are smooth creamed vegetable soups, and the light sharp-flavoured summer soups.

To begin a pot of soup you need a stock — a liquid base which will absorb the flavour of all the good things going into the pot. How do you get your stock? Do you make your own, or use a stock cube?

A busy person does not always have time to make stock in the old way, boiling up bones or vegetable trimmings, and may be short of materials, perhaps through purchasing the useful boneless cuts of meat and chicken available today. One handy idea in this situation, according to the nature of the soup you are planning to make, is to put a modest-sized piece of boiling beef, perhaps rib or shin, quite unconnected with the recipe, into the soup pot, just for flavour. It can be taken out and eaten later, perhaps shredded for a lunch sandwich filling. I sometimes do this to enrich the stock flavour for cock-a-leekie, which has a rather thin broth.

The stock cube is always coming under fire, being considered too salty, or too chemical-tasting, but probably you will add more salt anyway to a large pot of soup when doing a last check on the flavour.

1

And you will have so many tasty vegetables and perhaps a piece of meat in the pot that the exact flavour origin of the base stock is hidden. A stock cube can often leave you with a better end-flavour than if you had started off with water alone. Also, the cubes are low in fat, a fact appreciated by people on low calorie diets. Home-made stocks should be chilled and the hardened surface fat lifted away before use, a procedure for which one does not always have time. So, if you are a busy person and you like the flavour of the stock cube you have in mind for your next pot of soup, use it. Better still, have a look in your local health shop at the range of meat and vegatable stock cubes and flavourings made by manufacturers less well known than those on your supermarket shelf. Some of them are very good, made with careful attention to the principles of good health.

Cock-a-leekie

The prunes need not be eaten, but their presence in the stock cuts any bitterness from the leeks, and for some people the prunes are the highlight of the dish.

boiling fowl, about 3-3½ lb
3 pints beef stock or water
leeks, about 2 lb
2 prunes per serving, soaked
    overnight
salt and pepper

(sprig of parsley, bay leaf,
    few peppercorns, clove)
small piece boiling beef
    (optional)
chopped parsley to garnish

Clean and chop the leeks. Heat the beef stock and add the cleaned and trussed fowl to the pot, with half of the leeks. If using water instead of stock, add the herbs and spices tied in a square of cotton. Bring to the boil and skim for a few minutes until clear. Reduce heat and simmer until the bird is tender. This can take 2 hours or longer. Remove the bird and add the rest of the leeks and the prunes. Simmer for another half hour and check that the leeks are tender. Test the seasoning. Keep the breast meat of the bird for another meal, but chop a little of the other flesh into the broth. Take the best bit of the breast skin, roll it up and slice it into fine shreds to add to the pot. Serve with 2 prunes per person and sprinkle each bowl with chopped parsley.

If you have no beef stock to start the dish, or want a richer broth, cook a small piece of boiling beef along with the bird, but start it off about an hour before you put in the fowl, with a chopped onion and just enough water to cover the beef. Discard the onion when you start cooking the bird, and top up the water to cover.

Leek and tattie soup

1 lb leeks
½ lb potatoes
1 onion
1 oz butter

2 pints chicken stock
salt and pepper
cream to serve

Clean and chop the vegetables and cook gently in the butter in a soup pot, adding the stock and seasoning after 5 minutes. Cover and simmer for 20 minutes, checking that the potatoes are soft. Cool a little, then liquidise the soup or push it through a sieve. Return to the pot, add some hot water gradually to thin the soup to a good consistency, and reheat. Season to taste. Serve with a swirl of cream in each bowl.

Scotch broth

The old favourite. Mutton is not so easy to find now, but lamb or beef can be used instead.

1-1½ lb mutton scrag or
  middle neck of lamb
2 oz pearl barley
2 oz dried peas or 8 oz fresh
  shelled peas
1 onion, 1 leek, chopped
1 cup carrot, diced

1 cup turnip, diced
2 celery stalks, chopped
1 tablesp chopped parsley
salt and pepper
1 finely grated carrot,
  (optional)

some larger pieces of carrot and turnip
wedge of white cabbage

If using the dried peas, soak overnight, then drain. Wash the meaty bones and cut away as much fat as possible. Put in a soup pot and cover with 3 pints of water. Bring to the boil and skim several times for a few minutes until clear. Scald the barley, then add to the pot with the dried peas and simmer for half an hour. Add the chopped and diced vegetables and cook for 1½-2 hours, or until the meat is tender. Take out the bones and shred the meat from them. Taste and season the broth, and return the meat to the pot. The addition of a finely grated carrot at this point improves colour and flavour. If you are using fresh peas, add and cook for a minute or two. Skim the fat from the broth by drawing a piece of kitchen paper across the surface. Stir in the parsley just before serving.

If there is enough meat to make a separate course, add some larger pieces of carrot and turnip to the broth about 45 minutes before required, and the cabbage about 20 minutes before, to serve with the meat.

3

Hairst bree/Hotch potch

'Harvest broth'. The characteristic of this soup is the freshness of the young vegetables used. It is made in much the same way as Scotch broth, but the dried pulses are omitted, and syboes (spring onions) are generally used instead of onions.

1 lb scrag mutton or lamb, chicken, or beef	6 syboes
2-3 lb any young vegetables (peas, broad beans, turnips, carrots, etc.)	small cauliflower
	small lettuce
	salt and pepper
	chopped parsley to garnish

Put the meat into a soup pot. Cover with 4 pints salted water. Bring to the boil and skim. Dice all the vegetables, and add everything except the cauliflower and lettuce to the pot. Cook gently for 1 hour. Add the cauliflower and lettuce and simmer for a further 30 minutes. Shred the meat and return to the pot, discarding skin and bone. Check the seasoning. Stir in the parsley, and serve with buttered toast fingers.

Poacher's broth

1 rabbit, jointed	1 oz butter or margarine
2 onions, carrots, sticks of celery, roughly chopped	1 oz flour
good pinch nutmeg	¼ pint milk
12 peppercorns, crushed	1 egg yolk
salt and pepper	4 tablesp single cream or top-of-the-milk

Wash the rabbit joints and blanch briefly in boiling water in a soup pot. Drain. Cover with lightly salted water, bring to the boil, and skim. Add the vegetables and seasonings, and simmer for about 2½ hours, until the rabbit is tender. Strain, and discard the vegetables.* Return the broth to the pot, dice the meat from one of the joints, and add to the soup, keeping the rest of the meat for another meal. To thicken the soup, melt the butter in a small saucepan and cook the flour gently for a minute or two without browning. Add a little of the broth gradually, to obtain a thin sauce, then stir this into the pot. Whisk the egg yolk, milk, and cream together, and strain into the soup. Be careful not to let the soup boil after adding the cream, to avoid curdling.

* If a simpler flavour is preferred, the soup can be thickened with a puree of the cooked vegetables, rather than with the flour.

Note A tasty meal can be made with the cooked rabbit pieces. Remove the bones, egg-and-crumb the meat, and fry in a little hot butter until golden. Serve with a wedge of lemon, mashed potatoes or chips, and a juicy green vegetable.

Pork beanfeast

A thick soup-stew.

smoked ham shank, about 1 lb	½ lb pork belly slices
2 oz each, red kidney beans, butter beans, black-eye beans	2 pints chicken stock (use cube)
2 onions, carrots	4 oz fresh or frozen peas
2 sticks celery	pinch mixed herbs
1 red pepper	salt and pepper
	crusty bread, to serve

Soak the beans* and the shank overnight, in two separate bowls of water. Next day, drain the beans, cover with fresh water, and bring to the boil. Reduce heat and cook for 1 hour. Meanwhile, cut the pork slices into bite size pieces, discarding the rind, and brown them in their own fat in a small frypan. Clean and chop the vegetables and place them in a large casserole (8 pint) or a soup pot. Drain the shank and add to the vegetables. Add the browned pork pieces. Season with salt and pepper and a pinch of herbs. Pour in the stock. Put the lid on the casserole or pot and cook for 3 hours in oven (180°C/350°F/gas mark 4) or on top of the stove, adding a little more stock or boiling water if necessary, until the shank meat is tender. Remove the shank and shred the meat, discarding skin and bone. Stir the meat into the beans, add the peas, and adjust the seasoning. Serve with crusty bread.

SERVES 6-8

Leftovers can be liquidised or sieved and diluted to taste for later servings.

* **Note** It is important to follow the vendor's packet instructions for the preparation of red kidney beans before proceeding with the general method of the recipe. It is usually recommended that they are soaked for 18 hours then boiled in salted water for 15 minutes, before using in a recipe.

Ham and pea soup

A rib-sticking smoky soup with tender chunks of ham. Pulses (peas, beans and the like) are rich sources of protein and fibre.

a smoked ham shank, about 1-2 lb	few stalks of parsley
8 oz split peas	salt and pepper
1 onion, carrot, potato	pinch nutmeg

Soak the ham shank and split peas in separate bowls overnight. Next day drain, and discard the liquid. Put the shank and peas in a soup pan and cover with water — about 2 pints. Peel and chop the vegetables, and add to the pot with the parsley. Bring to the boil, skim, reduce the heat and simmer for 1½ hours. Take out the shank and sieve or liquidise the soup. Cut the meat from the bone and replace it in the soup. Season carefully, as the shank will still be a bit salty. Skim the fat from the soup with a sheet of kitchen paper. A pinch of nutmeg enhances the ham flavour. Serve with crusty bread.

Partan bree

Partans are large edible crabs.

1 medium partan, boiled
2 oz rice
1 pint milk
water or stock, made from
    shell
strip of lemon rind

bay leaf, few peppercorns,
    chopped onion
salt and white pepper
anchovy essence
¼ pint single cream

Crack all the claws and take out the meat, setting aside the pieces from the large claws. Scrape out the brown and white meat and cut up. If using a stock make one now from the shell and small claws. Put these in a polythene bag and tap with a rolling pin to break up. Put it all in a pan with a bay leaf, peppercorns, and chopped onion. Cut a thin strip of rind, about 2 inches long, from a lemon, avoiding the pith, and add to the pot with enough water to cover the shell pieces. Simmer for half an hour then strain the liquor through a fine sieve and discard the shell. Meanwhile cook the rice gently in the milk until tender — about 15 minutes — and stir in the chopped flesh. Sieve or liquidise. Return to the pan. Add the stock, or water, until you have the consistency you like. Season with salt and pepper and a drop or two of anchovy essence. Heat through and serve. Cream is usually added to this soup just before serving, but I prefer to offer it separately at the table, in a small jug.

Cheese and ale soup

1 oz butter
1 lb leeks, finely cut
1 oz flour
1 pint chicken stock
½ pint milk
¼ pint ale

8 oz mature Scottish cheddar
    cheese, grated
2 teasp mustard
salt and pepper
2 rashers streaky bacon,
    grilled and chopped

Melt the butter in a saucepan and cook the leeks gently for 10 minutes. Stir in the flour and cook 1 minute. Gradually add the chicken stock, milk and ale. Bring up to the boil, stirring continuously. Reduce the heat and stir in the cheese and mustard. Cover and simmer gently until the cheese has melted. Do not allow to boil again. Season to taste. Serve each bowl with a sprinkling of chopped bacon.

Skink soup

In Scotland, skink is a beef leg cut, shin of beef. It has an older meaning, 'a soup or potage of boiled shin of beef' (Scottish National Dictionary).

piece of skink, about 1 lb
marrow bone
1 lb mixed vegetables, peeled
and finely diced — onion,
carrots, turnip, potato,
celery, etc.

bay leaf
1 tablesp chopped parsley
salt and pepper

Put the meat and bone in a soup pot with the bay leaf, salt and pepper, and 2 pints of water. Bring to the boil, skim until clear, and cover. Reduce heat and simmer until the meat is tender, about 1½-2 hours. Remove the meat, discard the bone and cut the flesh into small pieces. Strain the stock, rinse the pan and return the liquid to the pot. Draw a piece of kitchen paper across the surface to lift away the fat. Add the vegetables and simmer about 40 minutes. Stir in the meat, check the seasoning and add a little more water if necessary for a good consistency. Sprinkle in the parsley just before serving.

The following recipe, Cullen skink, is a smoked haddock speciality and the only recipe that uses the term 'skink' with reference to fish.

Cullen skink

There is something of a cook's mystery as to how Cullen skink got its name, but as early as 1897 there was a version of the cure known as the 'Moray Firth pale cure haddock' (The Finnan Haddie, Cornwall, *Aberdeen, 1897), so that it does seem most likely that the famous fish soup originated in Cullen on the Moray coast.*

1 Finnan haddock
1 onion
1 pint milk
¼ cup single cream

1 oz butter
mashed potato
salt and pepper
little chopped parsley

Poach the haddock with a sliced onion in just enough water to cover, until the fish flakes easily. Remove the skin and bones from the fish, return them to the cooking liquid, and simmer for 30 minutes to obtain a well-flavoured stock. Strain, and replace stock in the rinsed pan. Heat the milk separately, then add to the stock. Stir in the flaked fish and enough mashed potato to give a creamy thickness. Season, stir in the cream and add the butter in little pieces to melt in small ribbons. Stir only lightly. Sprinkle with parsley. Eat with fingers of dry toast.

Summer tomato soup

A refreshing sharp-flavoured soup to make when tomatoes are plentiful in the shops or greenhouse. The recipe can be used for frozen tomatoes also.

1½-2 lb ripe tomatoes
2 onions
few bacon rinds
salt

1½ pints chicken stock,
home-made or made from
stock cube
pinch of sugar

Put bacon rinds in a soup pot. When hot, add the chopped onions and allow to colour slightly. Slice the tomatoes and add to the pot, stirring until the fat of the bacon is absorbed. Cover and allow the ingredients to cook gently in their own juices for about half an hour. Add the stock and simmer 15 minutes. Discard the rinds and push the soup through a sieve, or liquidise, then pour through a strainer to remove the seeds and scraps of tomato skin. Season with salt and a pinch of sugar. If the soup is too sharp to your taste, stir in a pinch of bicarbonate of soda to cut the acidity.

Kidney and tomato soup

A hearty winter soup.

4-6 oz piece of ox kidney
1 oz butter or margarine
2 oz broth mix (barley,
lentils, etc.)

1 onion, carrot, leek, potato,
diced
14 oz can of tomatoes
salt and pepper

Rinse the kidney. Melt the butter in a soup pot, and turn the vegetables in the hot fat. Cook gently for a few minutes. Chop the canned tomatoes, discarding any skin or tough bits, and add to the pan with the kidney and the broth mix. Cover with cold water. Bring to the boil, skim, then reduce heat to a simmer for 1½-2 hours. Remove the kidney, chop up the meat and return to the pan. To thicken the soup, take about a pint of the broth and vegetables out of the pot, and puree through a sieve or liquidiser. Return to the pot and stir.

Tomato and mushroom soup

Light and tasty, quick to make.

8 tomatoes, medium size
1 oz butter
2 tablesp corn oil
1 onion, chopped
1 clove of garlic

¼ lb mushrooms
2 tablesp tomato ketchup
1 tablesp Worcester sauce
1 pint beef stock (use a cube)
salt and pepper

Peel and crush the clove of garlic in a little salt, using the blade of a knife. Melt the butter and oil together in a soup pan, and fry the onion and garlic gently for 5 minutes. Meanwhile, drop the tomatoes into a bowl of boiling water for a minute. The skins will burst and can be easily pulled off. Chop the flesh and add to the pan with the ketchup, sauce and mushrooms. Cover and simmer for 5 minutes. Add the stock and seasoning. Simmer 20 minutes. If liked, serve with garlic croutons.

To make garlic croutons Melt a generous knob of butter in a pan, and stir in a peeled and crushed clove of garlic. Cut up a slice of bread into small dice, discarding the crust, and turn in the hot butter till golden. Serve at once, sprinkled in the bowls of soup.

Egg and lemon soup

One of the fringe benefits of a prize-winning holiday in Greece was the opportunity it gave me to sample new dishes, some of which I have been able to adapt and add to my own collection. In Greece this soup is a classic known as Avgholemono. Light and pleasantly tart, it is a happy choice to start a special meal.

2 eggs	2 pints chicken stock (from
1 lemon	cube)
1 oz butter	½ cup single cream
1 oz plain flour	salt and pepper
1 onion, chopped	

Melt the butter in a soup pot and soften the onion over a gentle heat, without browning. Remove the pan from the heat and stir in the flour. Cook gently for a minute, then add the stock gradually, stirring. Rub the lemon on the fine side of a grater and add the shreds of peel to the pan. Squeeze out the juice and add with the seasoning to the soup. Bring to the boil, then lower the heat and simmer for 15 minutes. Strain the soup, rinse the pan, and allow to cool a little. Beat the eggs in a large bowl and stir in the cream. Stir the lemon mixture gradually into the egg mixture, then return to the pot. Reheat gently before serving. Take care not to let it boil after adding the cream, or the soup will curdle and be spoiled.

Pumpkin soup

This golden soup is an American favourite, and a welcome addition to the northeast table. Pumpkins are of the same family as marrows and courgettes, and can be very large. A 1 lb slice is a useful amount for soup or a sweet pie (see page 48). You can also roast pumpkins, cut into fairly large chunks, round a meat joint in the same way as parsnips, or boil in lightly salted water and serve with a cheese sauce. Pumpkins are available in the Grampian area from late August.

slice of pumpkin, about
  1-1½ lb
1 onion, finely chopped
1 large potato, diced
1 oz butter
2 pints chicken stock (use
  cube)

salt and pepper
¼ teasp each of nutmeg,
  ginger and sugar
pinch cayenne, optional
¼ pint top-of-the-milk

Peel the pumpkin and cut into chunks. (If the pumpkin skin is tender there is no need to peel it.) Melt the butter in a soup pot and turn the vegetables in the hot fat, to coat. Cook gently for a few minutes, then add the stock and bring up to the boil. Skim, then reduce the heat and simmer for about 20 minutes until the vegetables are tender. Puree, return to the pot and add the seasonings. Stir in the top-of-the-milk. Be careful not to let the soup boil after the creamy milk is added, or it may curdle.

A swirl of soured cream is a delicious garnish for the soup, and can be simply made by stirring a little lemon juice into fresh cream. Alternatively, serve knobs of chilled butter coated with chopped parsley or chives.

Cream of oats soup

A personal favourite.

2 tablesp medium oatmeal
1 oz butter
1 onion, chopped
2 pints chicken stock (use 1
  cube)
2 rashers bacon

1 large cooking apple, peeled
  and cored
1 slice wholemeal bread
level teasp curry powder
top-of-the-milk, about half a
  cup

Melt the butter in a soup pan and cook the oatmeal and onion gently for a few minutes. Add the stock, chopped bacon, apple, bread and curry powder. Cover and simmer for an hour. Sieve or liquidise the soup. Adjust seasoning. Return the soup to the pan, stir in the creamy milk, and reheat without allowing it to come to the boil.

ℱish

GRAMPIAN IS the centre of the fishing industry in Scotland, with busy fishing ports all along its long coastline from Kincardine to the Moray Firth. Inland are great salmon rivers. An abundance of fish is part of the northeast heritage.

Despite the variety of fish caught, the northeast fish eater tends to have conservative tastes, preferring to make his choice from a few firm favourites, haddock and lemon sole being especially appreciated. He enjoys a piece of smoked fish, perhaps the pale golden Finnan haddock with the backbone on the right in the Aberdeen cure, or a golden cutlet with a poached egg on top. A piece of salmon is something of an occasional treat, and he admits to liking the rich flavour of salmon from a tin, but fresh salmon is now a sensible alternative to expensive meat.

Grampian has a fine record in the curing of fish, from the days of poor and slow road and sea travel, when ways had to be found for preserving surplus fish, for local use and for sending further afield for profit. From these early experiments come the fine cures we enjoy today, particularly the cold-smoked Finnan and the hot-smoked Arbroath smokie. It is still possible to buy some salted fish.

One characteristic shared by fish eaters along the Grampian seaboard is an expectation of perfect freshness in their fish. They

11

will label as 'rotten' a fish that most other people would consider perfectly edible. When the Grampian fish eater travels inland for an outing, he is less likely to choose fish from the high tea menu at an inland hotel, since, being so far from the sea, he thinks that it cannot possibly be fresh. Even among the coastal communities there are differences of opinion in judging freshness to the nose and palate, and a fish eater from the Broch (Fraserburgh), who can have his fish in a frying pan within a hour of a trawler coming into port, will often regard Aberdeen fish, eaten some hours after it left the Fish Market, as long past the peak of freshness.

COD

Cod in tomato

Canned tomatoes can also be used successfully in the recipe.

4 cod steaks or fillets, about 6 oz each	pinch cayenne pepper
2 onions, finely chopped	2 teasp brown sugar
1 oz butter or margarine	pinch mixed herbs
1 lb ripe tomatoes	1 teasp salt
2 teasp made mustard	1 tablesp chopped parsley

Preheat the over to 190°C/375°F/gas mark 5. Wash the fish and pat dry. Fry the onion gently in the butter until transparent. Skin the tomatoes by dropping them in a bowl of boiling water for a minute, when the skins can be pulled off easily. Arrange the fish in a buttered oven dish. Sprinkle the onions over the fish. Chop the tomatoes and place in a pan with all the seasonings and parsley, and heat through. Pour over the fish. Bake for 30-40 minutes, and test that the fish flakes easily. Serve with crusty bread.

DABS

Buttered dabs

Dabs are small flat fish, a species of flounder. They yield delicate little white fillets tasting much like sole, and are very popular in the northeast.

allow 3-4 fillets per person	lemon
butter	salt and pepper

Rub a knob of butter over a soup plate. Roll up the little fillets and arrange on the plate, Place a flake of butter on top of each fillet and season the fish with salt and pepper. Put the plate over a pan of simmering water, cover the fish with the pan lid and cook for 20-30 minutes till the fish flakes easily. Serve with mashed potatoes and a squeeze of lemon juice.

Dab pinwheels As a variation, spread the fillets with a stuffing before rolling up. A few served with a lemon wedge make an attractive appetiser or small fish course as part of a larger meal. Suggested stuffings — finely chopped mushrooms softened in hot butter and mixed with breadcrumbs, lemon juice, fine shreds of lemon peel, and parsley; prawns or crabmeat mashed with seasonings, lemon juice and a little melted butter. Secure fish with cocktail sticks while cooking.

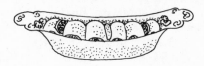

HADDOCK

The haddock is Grampian's favourite fish. A fish supper from the local 'chipper' will be a haddock supper, not the cod favoured in the south. The fish will be deep-fried in a crisp puffed-up batter of flour-and-water. Prepared at home, the fish is more usually coated in the popular 'golden crumbs' and either grilled or fried, with the deep-fat pan being used just for cooking the chips. To coat the fish, dip it in a saucer of a little milk with a pinch of salt mixed in — no need to waste an egg — and press into the crumbs to coat well. Season. Fry in hot corn oil or a knob of melted margarine, or grill, dotted with flakes of butter or margarine, or coated with oil. If you can organise a small squeezy plastic bottle kept filled with cooking oil to use for grilling, the fish can be sprayed with a light film of oil without the need to touch it. A brush will always lift some of the coating, however careful you are.

Haddock with orange

For each person
1 haddock fillet   flour for coating
1 small sweet orange   salt and pepper
melted butter

Preheat oven to 180°C/350°F/gas mark 4. Cut a square of foil for each fillet. Halve the orange. Squeeze the juice from one half and chop the flesh of the other half, discarding the peel. Melt a little butter in a small soup plate set over a pan of hot water — 1 oz will do for 4 fillets. Brush the fillet with melted butter, then dust with seasoned flour. Lay the fish on the square of foil, pour over the orange juice and add the chopped orange flesh. Close the parcel and bake for half an hour. The juice will thicken a little in the flour from the fish, forming a delicious sauce.

If liked, add a few peeled prawns to each parcel.

13

Cutlets in cream

Lightly smoked, skinned and filleted haddock are used in this recipe. Some fishmongers in Grampian have a smoke cure so light that the fish are barely coloured and have a delicate flavour necessary for this dish.

4 smoked haddock fillets	few capers
little butter	½ pint cream
4 oz mushrooms	12 black peppercorns

Preheat oven to 180°C/350°F/gas mark 4. Poach the haddock in water just to cover, for 5 minutes, to cook gently and draw out the excess saltiness. Drain, flake the fish and place it in a shallow buttered oven dish. Rinse the mushrooms, slice very finely and scatter over the fish with the capers. Pour the cream over to cover the fish. Put the peppercorns in a polythene bag and crush coarsely with a rolling pin. Scatter the black flakes over the cream. Bake for 10-12 minutes. A skin will form on top of the cream. Meanwhile heat the grill to high, and brown the top before serving. SERVES 2-3

Finnan croûtes

1 Finnan haddock	salt and pepper
1 oz grated cheese	pinch cayenne or paprika
1 tablesp cream or	4 croûtes
top-of-the-milk	tomato or cress to garnish
1 egg	

Mash the flesh of the haddock with a fork, discarding skin and bone, and cook gently in a pan with the cream, seasonings and cheese for a few minutes, until the cheese melts. Stir in the beaten egg and cook a little longer. Meanwhile make the croûtes. Cut circles from day-old bread with a pastry cutter or top of a cup, and fry gently in butter or dripping until golden. Pile the fish mixture on to the hot croûtes and garnish with a slice of tomato, or cress. SERVES 2

Arbroath smokies

Known as 'Tied Tailies', these are a speciality of the northeast — sweet haddock (up to 8 or even 10 oz) tied in pairs by the tails and smoked over oak or beech hardwood blocks. Sometimes other white fish are used. They are cleaned and salted, but not split open, so that they stay moist as they cook inside their skins, in the hot smoke. You can open them and eat them as they are or heat them by rubbing the skin with oil and grilling each side a few minutes.

For a simple supper dish take the flesh from the bone and stir in a hot pan with a nut of butter to just heat through. Pile on the top of softly scrambled eggs and serve with toast.

14

Smokie puffs

2 smokies
3 slices white bread
butter
3 eggs

3 tablesp thick cream
parmesan cheese or a little
    finely grated cheddar
salt and papper

Preheat over to 180°C/350°F/gas mark 4. Take the eggs from the fridge at least an hour before making up the dish so that the yolks are not ice cold. Split the smokie and take out the flesh, discarding skin and bone. Heat it through in a pan with a nut of butter. Trim the crusts from the bread and toast lightly till only just coloured. Allow to cook then spread one surface of each slice with butter, taking it right to the edges. Divide the smokie flesh between the slices, spreading it out. Crack the eggs and separate whites from yolks, putting all the whites in a large bowl and sliding a yolk onto the centre of each slice on top of the fish. Put a spoonful of cream over each yolk and sprinkle the cream only with a little parmesan or cheddar cheese. Season the egg whites lightly then whisk until thick and standing in peaks. Spoon over the yolks and fish, spreading it right to the edges of the toast. Bake for 10 minutes. Have the diners seated at table, and serve. The dish is so lightly cooked that it must be eaten immediately.

Note As a general guide to quantity, two 6 oz smokies will yield flesh for 3 servings. Multiply quantities as required.

Smokie flan

Pastry
4 oz plain flour
4 oz wheatmeal flour
2 oz lard
2 oz margarine

1 teasp mustard powder
1 teasp salt
fresh ground pepper
2 tablesp water

Filling
Arbroath smokie
1 onion, finely chopped
1 tablesp oil
2 oz cheddar cheese, grated

3 eggs, size 3
½ pint creamy milk
salt and pepper

To make pastry Turn on oven to heat to 200°C/400°F/gas mark 6. Stir the dry ingredients to mix, rub in the fats to the texture or breadcrumbs and bind the mixture with 2 tablespoons water. Roll out on a floured worktop, then use to line a 10-inch flan tin. Lightly prick the base with a fork. Line the pastry with greaseproof paper weighted with baking beans and bake the pastry case for 10 minutes. Remove greaseproof and beans and bake for a further 10 minutes. Remove from oven, and reduce heat to 180°C/350°F/gas mark 4.

To make filling Heat the oil in a small saucepan and cook the onion gently until softened but not browned. Meanwhile, open the smokie and take out the flesh, discarding the skin and bone. Scatter the flesh on the pastry base. Sprinkle in the cheese and the softened onion. Whisk the eggs into the milk with a dash of salt and a grind of pepper. Pour into the pastry case. Bake for 45 minutes until golden and set. Allow to cool for about 10 minutes before serving.

SOLE

Two ways with this northeast favourite.

Sole with capers Fry seasoned small filleted sole in hot butter. When tender, transfer from the pan to a hot serving plate. Add a little lemon juice, chopped parsley and a few capers to the butter remaining in the pan. Heat until the butter darkens slightly. Pour over the fish.

Sole with tongue Allow 2 single sole fillets per serving, roll up the fish and secure with cocktail sticks. Poach the fish in a seasoned mixture of fish stock (made from fish bones) and a little white wine or cider. Remove the fish from the stock and place on circles of tongue in a hot serving dish. Boil the stock in the pan to reduce to a glazing consistency, then add a knob of butter and a little cream to make a coating sauce. Add a few peeled prawns then pour over the fish.

CRAB

Crab tart

A tasty starter, party quiche, or suummer lunch dish, with salad. Can also be made with prawns.

shortcrust pastry (as on page 15), flavoured with a shake of cayenne pepper and 1 oz grated cheddar cheese
12 oz cooked crab meat, fresh or canned

5-oz carton cottage cheese
2 teasp lemon juice
3 eggs
½ teasp Worcestershire sauce
pinch salt

Stir the cayenne into the flour. Rub in the margarine then stir in the grated cheddar before binding the mixture with water. Line the flan tin with the shortcrust pastry. Bake blind as described for the Smokie flan. Spread the crab meat (or prawns, or a mixture of the two) on the pastry. Beat together the eggs, salt, sieved cottage cheese, lemon juice and sauce (or, if you have a liquidiser, spin these ingredients till smooth), then pour over the crab meat. Bake at 190 C/375 F/gas mark 5 for 40 minues, until set. Serve warm or cold.

WHITE FISH (any kind)

Quenelles

These are light savoury dumplings.

8 oz white fish	1 egg
2 oz breadcrumbs	1 tablesp cream
1 oz butter	2 tablesp lemon juice
¼ pint fish stock or milk	salt and pepper

Mash the fish until smooth. Melt the butter, add the stock and crumbs and heat gently until the liquid is absorbed. Stir in the egg, cream, lemon juice and seasoning. Using two dessert spoons first dipped in boiling water, scoop out ovals of the mixture. Poach gently for 15 minutes in a shallow pan of boiling water or a light stock, held at a gentle simmer. Drain briefly on kitchen paper. Arrange the quenelles round the edge of a serving dish. Coat with hollandaise sauce (see p. 23). Fill the centre of the dish with fresh green peas, broad beans or sweetcorn.

Fish cake

A tasty fish cake is appreciated as a change from a fry, grill or bake. It is often made with cooked leftovers, or second-day fish. With his fine nose for freshness, the Grampian fish eater prefers second-day fish in a made-up dish.

1 lb cooked white fish	salt and pepper
1 lb cooked potatoes,	flour for coating
seasoned and mashed with	oil
a nut of butter	lemon wedges
1 tablesp chopped parsley	

Combine fish, potatoes and parsley. Season to taste. Pat into one large cake and dust with flour to coat. Heat oil in a pan and fry the cake slowly, browning on both sides. Cut into quarters and serve with lemon wedges.

Fish balls As a variation, form the mixture into balls about walnut size or smaller, egg-and-crumb them and fry in a hot fat or oil until golden. Drain on kitchen paper, then serve them hot with a spicy sauce as part of a main meal, or on cocktail sticks with Mary Rose sauce, as an appetiser or a cocktail snack.

Mary Rose sauce Mix together equal quantities of cream, tomato ketchup and mayonnaise. Add Worcester sauce to taste. This is a useful seafood sauce for general use, and particularly for shellfish.

Kromeskies

8 oz cooked white fish
12 thin back bacon rashers
1 oz butter
1 oz flour
¼ pint fish stock or milk
1 egg yolk or 1 tablesp cream

salt and pepper
lemon juice
coating batter and hot oil for
frying
lemon wedges, to serve

Cut up the fish very finely, discarding skin and bone. Melt the butter and cook the flour gently for a few minutes without letting it colour. Beat in the liquid gradually and cook gently until thickened. Draw from the fire and whisk in the egg yolk or cream, and stir in the fish, salt and pepper, and lemon juice to taste. Turn out of the pan and allow to cool. Divide into 12 pieces and form into small rolls. Wrap each one in a piece of bacon, securing with a cocktail stick if necessary. Dip in the coating batter and fry in hot oil until golden. Remove the sticks and serve the kromeskies hot, with a wedge of lemon.

Coating batter Stir 6 oz self-raising flour with 1 teaspoon salt and ½ teaspoon baking powder. Mix with enough water to give the consistency of double cream, and beat until smooth. Leave for an hour before using.

HERRING

Herring in oatmeal

herring, cleaned and filleted
oatmeal
salt and pepper

dripping, or butter and oil
used together

Wipe the herring and pat very dry with a soft tea towel. Avoid washing the fish if possible. Press the herring into the oatmeal, coating as thickly as possible. Sprinkle generously with salt and pepper. Melt the fat in a large frying pan till very hot. Butter gives a lighter taste than the traditional dripping but needs a little oil to prevent it from scorching. Put in the fish, skin side first. Fry on both sides until brown, turning carefully as they break easily. Serve piping hot with mashed potatoes and buttered oatcakes and vinegar to sprinkle over the fish.

Soused herring

6 herring, cleaned and
filleted
2 bay leaves
6 cloves
6 black peppercorns
small onion, sliced

¼ pint cider vinegar
¼ pint water
pinch nutmeg
salt and pepper

Scrape the skin of the herring from tail to head to remove any loose scales, wash the fish and pat dry on kitchen paper. Season with salt and pepper. Roll them up tightly, tail to head, skin side out, and lay them close together in a shallow ovenproof dish. Tuck the bay leaves, cloves and peppercorns in between them. Sprinkle a pinch of nutmeg over the fish and scatter the onion slices on top. Mix the vinegar and water together and pour over just enough to cover the fish. Cover with foil and bake for 45 minutes at 180°C/350°F/gas mark 4. Store in the fridge. Serve cold with salad and brown bread and butter.

Malt vinegar can be used but has a harsher flavour.

MACKEREL

Spiced mackerel salad

Plump fillets of mackerel, smoked and spiced with mustard seed and crushed black peppercorns are becoming very popular in the northeast, and make a satisfying light meal.

2 fillets spiced smoked mackerel	French dressing
	1 hard boiled egg, sliced
3 oz long grain rice	2 tomatoes
2 oz fresh peas, cooked	lettuce leaves
2 oz sweetcorn	gooseberry curd to serve

Cook the rice in boiling salted water until tender. Drain and rinse with cold water, then mix with the peas and sweetcorn. Moisten with French dressing to taste, and season. Divide the egg slices, salad and rice mixture between two plates and top with the mackerel fillets cut into two or three pieces. Serve with a spoonful of gooseberry curd (p. 77) or a traditional rhubarb sauce, brown bread and butter, or oatcakes.

SERVES 2

Rhubarb sauce Cook 8 oz washed and diced rhubarb gently in 2 tablespoons water until soft. Mix ½ oz cornflour to a paste with a little water and blend into the rhubarb. Bring to the boil and cook, stirring, until smooth and thick. Allow to cool.

Smoked mackerel spread Mash a fillet of plain or spiced smoked mackerel with 2 oz of butter, 1 tablespoon cream and a good squeeze of lemon juice. Taste, and adjust seasoning. Serve with brown bread and butter, oatcakes, or toast.

SALMON

Salmon should never be overcooked. Although it is an oily fish, it will be dry and chewy if cooked too long. If you are using a fish that has been frozen, it must be completely thawed to avoid a raw centre to the cooked fish. There are several ways of cooking whole salmon and smaller cuts. One of the best, and simplest, is the old Scottish poaching method which will give firm, moist flesh. It can be used for any size of fish or fish piece. It does not matter if you do not own a fish kettle, but if you have a whole fish or a rather large cut, it helps to put something on the bottom of the pan that will help you to lift it out easily afterwards. This could be a cake rack, perhaps, or the grill rack from the cooker, or the trivet from a pressure cooker. Tie string to the side edges of the rack, or pass a sling of folded aluminium foil under the rack, and let the ends hang over the top edge of the pot while the fish is cooking, so that you can pull up the rack later.

To serve cold

Put the whole fish, or fish piece, in the pot, using a rack if it is large. Pour in enough cold water to cover the fish by about 1 inch. Salt the water lightly and add 1 tablespoon of vinegar or lemon juice. Bring slowly to the boil so that the fish heats up gently, right to the centre, and the skin does not burst. Immediately the water reaches boiling point, reduce the heat to a gently quivering simmer. The water should not be bubbling around the fish. Cover and simmer the fish for exactly 5 minutes. Remove the pot immediately from the heat and allow the fish to cool in the poaching fluid till completely cold. The larger the fish or fish piece, the more water there will be in the pan, and the longer it will take to cool down, so that the method adapts itself naturally according to the size of the fish. The slow cooling process is part of the cooking procedure, and the fish must be left until it is cold. The flesh firms up as it cools, so that the fish can be lifted quite easily out of the pot. Drain carefully, cover the fish and store in the fridge until required.

To serve hot or cold

If you are serving the salmon hot, the poaching process has to be completed in one stage, the cooking time allowance being calculated from the moment that the water comes to boiling point. Turn down immediately to a gentle simmer, cover and cook for 10 minutes per pound. Test with a skewer. Pull up the fish kettle strainer, or your improvised rack, if using, and drain the fish thoroughly, with a soft tea-towel over the top to keep it hot, before sliding it carefully from the rack to the serving dish. Alternatively, the fish can be covered and chilled for cold serving.

Some cooks like to add other flavourings to the poaching liquid. This is not necessary, as salmon is a rich and full-flavoured fish, but it is a matter of personal preference. The most I would ever add is perhaps a finely chopped shallot and a strip of lemon rind.

Cooking a tail cut

A recipe for a medium-size tail cut, which uses a combination of poaching and steaming.

Wipe the fish with kitchen paper and place it on a soup plate, lightly buttered to prevent the skin sticking to the plate. Pour in boiling water to come about halfway up the fish, add a little salt and a tablespoon of vinegar. Put the plate over a pan of boiling water without letting the water touch the underside. Cover the plate with the pan lid, or another plate, reduce the steamer heat to a simmer, and cook the fish for about half an hour, turning the tail piece carefully halfway through the cooking time. Test with the point of a knife and make sure the fish flakes easily. Remove the pot from the heat, and leave the whole arrangement as it is until completely cold. Lift the plate, tilt carefully and pour away the cooking liquid. Store in a cold place until required.

The advantage of this method is that very little of the flavour and the natural juices from the fish are lost in the small amount of cooking liquid surrounding the fish.

Cooking individual slices

There are other ways of cooking salmon which are suitable for the popular individual sliced cuts — steaks and cutlets — so that they retain their natural juices.

Steaming Steam on a lightly buttered and covered soup plate over a pan of simmering water. Season the fish with a little salt and lemon juice. The cooking time for a cut ¾-1 inch thick will be 20-30 minutes. Eat hot. For cold serving, it is better to use oil for cooking, as butter becomes solid when cold.

Grilling *Grill on the rack* Season the steaks, dot with butter and grill 10 minutes each side under a medium heat, for cuts about 1 inch thick, basting with the pan juices as they cook.
Grill in the pan For 4 steaks, melt 2 oz butter in the pan under a medium grill. Season the steaks, dust them lightly with flour, and turn them in the hot butter. Grill them about 8 minutes each side, depending on their thickness, and baste with the pan juices as they cook. For a tasty thin crust, sprinkle a little more flour over them. Turn up the grill and cook briefly to brown.

Poaching in foil *For cold serving* Put each slice of fish on a large square of foil which has been brushed with oil. Enclose the fish loosely but twist the foil edges to make a watertight parcel. Place the parcels in a pan, cover with cold water. Bring to the boil, reduce immediately to a simmer and cook for exactly 5 minutes. Remove the pan from the heat and leave the parcels in the water until completely cold.

Baking in foil *For hot serving* Butter a square of foil and enclose all the slices in one parcel, twisting the foil edges to make secure. For the average 8 oz slices, bake for half an hour at 140°C/275°F/gas mark 1.

Smoked salmon

Smoked salmon is so expensive that probably the best way to serve it is as an appetiser. Cut into wafer-thin strips, roll up and serve two or three per person with cold scrambled eggs, served on a croûte. The eggs should be well seasoned.

Croûtes With a scone cutter or the rim of a cup, cut circles from day-old bread. Spread thinly with butter on each side, lay on a baking sheet and bake 15-20 minutes in a moderate oven (180°C/350°F/gas mark 4). Use when cold.

Scrambled eggs Enrich the scrambled eggs for this special serving by using the chef's trick of adding an extra yolk to every three eggs used, with ½ oz butter and a tablespoon of thick cream. Season and cook over a gentle heat till thick and creamy. Turn into a bowl and allow to become cold. If you allow it to cool in the pot the texture will be spoiled as the hot pan continues to cook the eggs.

TROUT

Trout is much improved if lightly salted and allowed to lie overnight. Next day, wipe the fish, split it open and remove the bone. Dip in milk and press into oatmeal to coat thickly. Fry in smoking hot lard or a mixture of oil and butter for a few minutes each side. Serve with butter and a wedge of lemon, or a mustard sauce.

Mustard sauce

4 egg yolks	salt and pepper
1 teasp made mustard	pinch caster sugar, to taste
2 teasp horseradish sauce	1 tablesp chopped parsley
3 tablesp salad oil	

Whisk the yolks, mustard and horseradish sauce lightly together in a small bowl. Gradually whisk in the oil a little at a time. Season to taste with the sugar, salt and pepper. Stir in the parsley.

SOME GARNISHES FOR FISH

Shaped croutons Cut about 6 small shapes from each of several slices of white bread, using pastry cutters or a bottle cap. Fry in a mixture of oil and butter till golden.

Fried parsley A chef's garnish, bright green and crisp. Fry sprigs of parsley in hot oil for half a minute. Drain on kitchen paper.

Lemon basket Cut a simple basket shape from a lemon. Mark a centre strip ¼ inch wide across the top of the lemon. Cut away the lemon from both sides of the strip, and remove the flesh from under the handle.

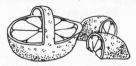

SAUCES FOR SALMON AND OTHER FISH

Salmon needs a sauce to accompany it. Melted butter, lightly seasoned and with a little lemon juice added, is a simple and delicious accompaniment to hot salmon. The butter should first be clarified by skimming the white solids after melting it. An hollandaise sauce is an alternative choice. Cold cuts are best served with a lemony mayonnaise. Hollandaise is a cooked sauce based on eggs and butter. Mayonnaise is uncooked, a sauce based on eggs and oil. Both are worth the little bit of care needed to make them, and can be used for many other dishes besides fish.

Hollandaise

Blender/Processor

2 egg yolks
pinch salt
3 oz butter

2 teasp lemon juice or cider vinegar

Warm the goblet by filling with hot water. Drain and dry. Put in the egg yolks with the salt. Heat the butter until very hot but not coloured, and add the lemon juice or vinegar. Switch on the machine and pour in the butter in a slow stream through the hole in the lid. Stop as soon as it is all beaten in. Spoon out into a warmed bowl and serve at once. It can be kept warm for a short time by standing the bowl in a larger container of hot water.

By hand

2 egg yolks
4 tablesp cream
pinch salt

3 oz butter
2 teasp lemon juice or cider vinegar

Heat the butter without letting it colour and add the lemon juice or vinegar. Beat the egg yolks with the cream and salt, then place the bowl

23

over a pan of very hot but not boiling water. Stir until the mixture thickens, then add the butter mixture in small amounts, stirring well between each addition. While working, take the bowl from the heat from time to time to keep the mixture from overheating. Serve.

Mayonnaise

Home-made mayonnaise is so superior to shop-bought that it is worth learning how to make it. For the acid element use lemon juice, cider vinegar or white wine vinegar. Malt vinegar is not suitable because of its harshness. For the oil, corn or a mixture of corn and olive oil, is suitable. Ingredients must be at warm room temperature.

Blender/Processor

1 whole egg	1 tablesp cider vinegar or
1 egg yolk	lemon juice
pinch salt	½ pint corn oil (or 50% corn,
pinch dry mustard	50% olive)
pinch caster sugar	

A whole egg has to be added to the basic recipe because most blender/processor blades are fixed too high above the base of the goblet to whip the single egg yolk properly. Place the whole egg, egg yolk and seasonings in the goblet. Blend. Add the vinegar or lemon juice and blend again. Add the oil to the goblet in small batches, blending after each addition, until it is all mixed in. Check seasoning. If it is too thick, add one tablespoon boiling water.

By hand

1 egg yolk	1 tablesp cider vinegar or
pinch salt	lemon juice
pinch dry mustard	¼ pint corn oil (or 50% corn,
pinch caster sugar	50% olive)

Put the egg yolk, seasonings and 1 teaspoon cider vinegar or lemon juice in a bowl and beat well with a whisk. Add half the oil drop by drop, a thin stream, whisking hard. This will take about 10 minutes. Stir in the remaining vinegar or lemon juice, a little at a time, until the mayonnaise is like thick cream. If too thick, beat in a tablespoon of boiling water.

Herbs of your choice can be added to give a green mayonnaise, e.g. parsely or chives.

Avocado sauce

For a mature late-season salmon, try an avocado sauce for a modern approach. Mash or puree a very ripe avocado with salt and pepper and a little lemon juice. Stir in a spoonful of the home-made mayonnaise. Serve immediately as it discolours eventually. The green sauce is an attractive foil to the flesh of the salmon.

Beef & Venison

THE GRAMPIAN meat eater likes a nice bit of beef. He is a mince and tattie man, and he expects his mince to be well made with a rich thick gravy. On a night on the town, his likely choice is a steak. Venison, well known in country districts, is less so in town, but I think that in the future this fine meat is going to become more popular. It is already being successfully semi-farmed, in protected environments, with most of the meat going to Continental markets. In time, a greater share is bound to reach our local tables. It is lean meat, wholesome and free from artificial growth-promoters.

BEEF

Grampian is famed for the fine quality of its home-grown beef. For many northeast folk, and visitors too, the highlight of a special meal is a juicy steak, perfectly cooked to their exact preference. The most popular grilling cuts locally are fillet, sirloin, T-bone and rump, with rump tending to be preferred as having, it is said, more flavour. Rump steak is a little less tender than the other three cuts and should be beaten before cooking.

25

Grilled rump steak

Allow steaks of 6-8 oz weight, ¾ inch thick, per person. Rump steak has a rim of fat along one edge. Snip this to prevent the steak curling up during cooking, but do not cut if off as it helps to keep the meat moist, even though you may prefer not to eat it. About an hour before cooking, beat the steak firmly with a rolling pin or meat mallet to tenderise it but take care not to over-beat it. If you like garlic, rub a clove over each side of the meat. Brush the meat with oil, shake freshly ground black pepper over it, and leave to rest. No salt, as this draws out the meat juices and toughens the steak.

To grill Turn on the grill and allow time to come to a fierce heat — about 15 minutes. Grill the steak 1 minute each side to seal the cut sides. Turn down the heat. Then cook the steak for the correct length of time for the way you like it done.

rare	2 minutes each side
medium rare	3
well done	4

Serve the steaks without adding salt, and allow your guests to season the meat to their taste, at the table.

Savoury butters

Serve the steaks with a pat of savoury butter to melt on top of the hot meat. When making up the butters, allow 4 oz of butter for a 4-person serving, add the flavourings, shape into a roll about 1 inch in diameter, wrap in foil or greaseproof paper, and chill in the fridge until required. Serve very cold, sliced in pats. They can also be served with fish, chops, liver, chicken and as a spread in a cheese scone.

Parsley butter   1 tablesp chopped parsley, salt and black pepper, 2 teasp lemon juice

Mustard butter   1 tablesp French mustard, 2 teasp lemon juice

Chive butter   2 tablesp chopped chives, salt and black pepper, 2 teasp lemon juice

Garlic butter   2 crushed cloves garlic, salt and black pepper, 1 teasp chopped parsley, 2 teasp lemon juice

Gaelic steak

For the Gaelic steak variation, add 2 tablespoons cream and 2 tablespoons whisky to the grill pan juices. Season with salt and fresh milled black pepper. Garnish with watercress.

26

Spiced beef

A savoury treat for the Christmas table, or a buffet, using Scotch brisket, the northeast favourite. This recipe omits the traditional use of saltpetre, the preservative which gave pickled meat its pink colour. It is no longer sold by chemists, and best avoided as a form of nitrate. This recipe is suitable for a joint of 4 lb or less, to be eaten within a week. Use sea or rock salt rather than table salt, which has chemicals added to keep it free-running that are best kept out of the spicing.

4 lb boned and rolled brisket	2 tablesp soft brown sugar
2 bay leaves	1 teasp ground allspice
1 teasp ground cinnamon	1 teasp black peppercorns
10 cloves	1 teasp sea or rock salt

Start this dish a week before you require it. It is easy to do and needs only a few minutes attention each day. Mix the spicing and ingredients and crush with a pestle (or the end of a rolling pin). Put into a large dish and roll the meat in the spice mixture, pressing well in. Cover with foil. Store in the fridge for 5 days, turning the meat daily in the sticky spice mixture. The sugar in the mix keeps the surface of the meat soft. When ready, take the joint out of the spicing and wipe off the excess — do not wash the meat. Pre-heat the oven to 150°C/300°F/gas mark 2. Lay the joint on a piece of foil, big enough to wrap into a parcel of double thickness. Place in a large casserole with a tight-fitting lid and add a pint of boiling water, covering the dish with foil before putting on the lid. Cook for 4 hours (1 hour per lb). At the end of the cooking time, take out of the oven and set aside in a cold place (not the fridge) for 3 hours. Open up and pour away the liquid. Unwrap the meat and squeeze it into a foil-lined tin a little too small for it — a tea-loaf tin is ideal. Cover with foil and weight it — bags of sugar, or tins, make good weights for pressing. Put in the fridge. The surface of the meat will dry to a thin brown spicy layer.

Serve sliced with other meats, with pickles, and in sandwiches. Keep the meat well wrapped in storage, to keep it moist.

Rumpsteak hamburger

An American way with a nice bit of Aberdeen Angus. The meat is first ground (minced).

Basic Recipe

2 lb ground steak	½ teasp salt
1 tablesp Worcester sauce	½ teasp crushed black
1 tablesp finely chopped	peppercorns
parsley	1 tablesp meat stock

Combine all the ingredients and pat out into 6 flat cakes, handling lightly to avoid compacting the meat. This helps to ensure it cooks properly to the centre. Grill or fry 3-5 minutes each side, according to how well done you like them. Serve in a split soft bun, or as a main meal with vegetables. MAKES 6

Serving variations

 Lay a slice of cheddar cheese on the top of the burger, after cooking the first side and turning.

 Make up the burger with a piece of blue cheese, camembert, brie or Lymeswold enclosed in the centre, before cooking.

 Add a heaped tablespoon of sesame seeds to the basic mixture.

 Serve topped with soured cream and dill (a hardy herb, easily grown, with a slightly aniseed flavour). Blanch the dill leaves in boiling water for 1 minute before patting dry and chopping. Stir into the cream.

 Soured cream topping flavoured with a pinch of chilli or mustard.

 Top with skinned tomatoes, heated through and well seasoned with salt, pepper and a pinch of chilli powder.

Frying steak and Minute steak

These are cooks' terms for any thin cut (¼-½ inch thick) of good quality boneless steak that will be tender to eat when quickly grilled or fried. Pan-frying is better and helps keep the meat juicy. Snip the edges to stop the meat curling up, and add salt only after cooking, to prevent toughness.

Minute steak rolls

4 thin minute steaks
4 oz fresh breadcrumbs
1 tablesp chopped parsley
1 tablesp chopped chives (or
  spring onion)

1 oz grated parmesan or
  cheddar cheese
black pepper

Beat steak as thin as possible with a rolling pin. Mix together the other ingredients and spread a little on each steak. Fold in each side, then roll up the steak. Secure each steak with two cocktail sticks. Brush with melted butter or a little oil and grill for a few minutes till cooked. Serve with salad. SERVES 2-3

To ensure that the meat remains tender do not add salt until the meat is cooked.

28

Fried beef and rice

This recipe makes a small quantity of expensive meat into a substantial dish.

8 oz frying steak	2 oz butter
seasoned flour	1 clove garlic, optional
1 egg	1 tablesp lemon juice
golden crumbs for cooking	several sprigs of parsley
2 oz butter + 1 tablesp oil	salt and black pepper
4 oz long grain rice	

Cut the steak into bite-sized pieces (about 2 inch square). Dip in flour, shake off the excess, then egg-and-crumb the pieces. Melt the butter and oil together in a frypan. When hot add the pieces and cook gently, turning several times, till brown and cooked through. Add a little more butter and oil to the pan if required during cooking. Meanwhile, bring a pot of salted water to the boil, and cook the rice for 7 minutes or until tender. Drain and keep the rice hot on a covered, buttered soup plate in a low oven, or over a pan of hot water. Mash the butter with the lemon juice, finely chopped parsley leaves and seasoning. Peel and crush the clove of garlic, if using, with the rounded end of a knife dipped in a little salt. Work it into the parsley butter. Divide into two pieces.

SERVES 2

To serve　Arrange the rice on two hot dinner plates in rounded heaps. 'Bury' a piece of the savoury butter in the centre of each. Arrange the fried beef pieces on top of the rice. Garnish with a slice of lemon and a parsley sprig.

CASSEROLE CUTS

Casserole meats — skirt, spaul, plate and other cuts — are best cooked in a small amount of liquid. Do not brown them first. This seals the fibres and makes the meat difficult to tenderise. Do not coat with flour, for the same reason. Add potatoes diced very small for a natural thickener. They will break up during the long cooking.

Spaul
Spaul is popular in Grampian. It is good-quality stewing meat from between the fore rib and neck area. It is usually sold sliced and can be casseroled in exactly the same way as ox skirt, in a dish or in foil. Use a minimum of liquid to conserve the meat juices.

Plate
Plate is lean meat from the shoulder, sold cut into neat slabs. Cook as skirt and spaul, but leave in one piece. When cold, it slices like roast meat and is excellent sandwich meat.

Ox skirt

This inexpensive cut, tender and rich in flavour, is often overlooked when choosing casserole meat. Skirts are long, thin pieces from inside the rump, flank or rib area. If you are stocking up a freezer ask for a few skirts to be included in the order. It is best to judge by eye how big a skirt you will need for the number of servings, as they differ in size. Butchers always have them in stock, but seldom on display, so you will probably have to ask for it.

1 or 2 ox skirts	1 stick celery, diced
1 onion, diced	meat stock cube
1 carrot, diced	pepper

Preheat oven to 180°C/350°F/gas mark 4. Cut off the 'waistband' of the skirt(s), and cut the skirt meat into sections about 3 inches wide, discarding the membranes. Lay the pieces overlapping in a shallow oven dish. Scatter over the vegetables. Dissolve the stock cube in about half a pint of hot water: pour over the meat, using only just enough to cover. Season with pepper. Cover closely with foil, and bake until tender (about an hour). Check the level of the stock about halfway through the cooking time. Test the seasoning. Serve hot with mashed potatoes.

Cold left-over pieces make neat and tender fillings for lunchtime sandwiches. Add a little pickle if liked.

Stuffed ox skirt

An old country recipe.

1 ox skirt	turnips, diced
carrots, diced	

Stuffing

4 oz medium oatmeal	2 oz chopped suet
1 small onion, finely chopped	salt and pepper

Preheat the over to 180°C/350°F/gas mark 4. Each side of the skirt meat is covered with a tough membrane. Insert the point of a knife at the open end of the skirt and gently pull the membrane loose from the meat, but leaving it attached at the 'waistband'. Turn the skirt over and do the same on the other side. Make up the stuffing. Put half of the stuffing on one side of the meat and pull the membrane back into place, enclosing the stuffing. Turn the skirt over and do the same on the other side. The meat is now sandwiched between two layers of stuffing, with the membranes on the outside. Sew up the open edges of the skirt membranes to hold in the stuffing. Put the prepared skirt into a deep oven dish with the vegetables and cover with water. Season. Cover and bake for two hours. Remove from oven to a serving dish and slice into portions to serve with the vegetables. If liked, use the cooking liquid to make gravy, first skimming off the fat.

Victoria steak

This delicious recipe comes from the 1935 edition of The Aberdeen Cookery Book *(Aberdeen School of Domestic Science).*

1 lb thin lean steak cut in one piece	¾ pint stock
1 oz dripping	salt and pepper
1 oz flour	2 oz chopped smoked ham for garnish

Stuffing

2 oz breadcrumbs	pinch mixed herbs
1 teasp chopped parsley	salt and pepper
grated rind of 1 lemon	egg yolk to bind
1 oz chopped ham	

Beat out the meat into a neat square. Make up the stuffing, lay it on the meat and roll up. Tie with string at intervals. Brown in hot dripping, add the stock and salt and bring up to boiling point. Skim, and reduce heat to a simmer. Cook for about 2 hours until the meat is tender. Thicken the gravy with flour. Remove the string, and serve the roll sliced with the strained gravy, and garnish with chopped ham.

MINCE DISHES

Minced collops

An easy dish for a novice cook.

1 lb steak mince	little oatmeal
¼ pint water	salt and pepper
1 onion, finely chopped	4 eggs
1 meat stock cube	4 slices bread
Worcester sauce	

Put the empty saucepan over a good heat, then with a wooden spoon stir the mince briskly on the hot pan base till browned in its own fat. Break up any lumps. Add the onion, water, crumbled stock cube, salt and pepper and a good dash of Worcester sauce. Cover and cook over a low temperature for half an hour, adding a little more hot water if necessary. Thicken by stirring in a light sprinkling of oatmeal. Check the seasoning. Meanwhile poach 4 eggs in a pan containing 1 inch of lightly salted simmering water, and toast 4 slices of bread. Put the mince on a hot platter (heat it by pouring boiling water on it then drying it), nestle the poached eggs into the meat and cut each slice of toast into 8 triangles with kitchen scissors. Arrange the snippets of toast round the edge of the dish.

Savoury sponge pudding

An attractive way to serve mince. It is a good-tempered dish that will not spoil if kept waiting.

1 lb steak mince
1 small onion, diced
meat stock cube

Worcester sauce
little oatmeal
salt and pepper

Topping
5 oz SR flour
2 oz margarine

2 eggs

Cook the mince as in the previous recipe, season, and thicken slightly. Turn into an ovenproof dish. Now make the topping. Pre-heat the oven to 190°C/375°F/gas mark 5. Rub the margarine into the flour until like fine breadcrumbs. Mix to a soft dough with the eggs. Spread over the meat. Bake for 45 minutes until the savoury sponge topping is nicely browned. Serve with green peas.

Aberdeen meat roll

Basic Recipe
½ lb steak mince
¼ lb streaky bacon
thick slice of bread
1 egg

½ cup water
salt and pepper
golden crumbs for coating

Cut up the bacon finely with a pair of kitchen scissors. Grate the bread into crumbs. Mix meat, bacon, crumbs, egg, water and seasoning in a bowl and squeeze it all together by hand. Pack the meat into a stone meat roll jar which has been rinsed out with cold water and left wet. Cover the top with foil or greaseproof paper, tying it on securely. Place in a pot of simmering water, cover, and steam for 1½ hours. Turn the meat roll out to stand upright on a soup-plate, and drain away the liquid from the plate, supporting the meat roll with a fish slice. Press the top of the roll gently to squeeze out excess liquid. (The liquid cools to a savoury jelly — use it for stock.) When cold, roll it in golden crumbs to coat. Serve sliced with salad.

Variation Make up a double quantity of the mixture. Pack half of it into a 2 lb loaf tin, and lay a line of hard-boiled eggs along the centre of the meat. Pack the rest of the mixture on top of the eggs and level the top. Cover with foil and bake in a moderate oven (180°C350°F/gas mark 4) for 1½-2 hours, standing the tin on a shallow baking tin holding about an inch of hot water. When cooked, turn out the meat loaf, drain off the stock, and crumb when cold. Cooked chicken or ham can be used in place of eggs.

Tasty snack meal Cut slices one inch thick from the roll. Egg and crumb them thickly. Fry gently in a knob of hot margarine until browned and hot through. Serve with a poached egg and fried tomatoes.

Sunshine meat roll

This recipe was created using Aberdeen meat roll as the starting point, and won first prize in the national final of the 1982 Green Giant / City Cook of the Year contest. It was demonstrated on Grampian ITV's Sign Hear *programme in August 1983.*

12 oz steak mince
6 oz minced pork
2 medium onions
1 clove garlic, peeled and
  crushed
2 oz mushrooms
small can sweetcorn
1 egg

2 oz fresh breadcrumbs
2 tablesp milk
good pinch mixed herbs
1 tablesp chopped parsley
1 teasp horseradish sauce
salt and pepper
1½ oz margarine

For glaze
4 tablesp tomato ketchup
½ meat stock cube

1 heaped tablesp mustard
  powder

Pre-heat oven to 180°C/350°F/gas mark 4. Soften the finely chopped onion and crushed clove of garlic in the margarine in a pan. Do not allow to brown. Mix the meats in a large bowl with the egg, milk, crumbs, half the onion mixture, herbs, horseradish, parsley, a level teaspoon salt and a good shake of pepper. Squeeze all together thoroughly with your hands. Put mixture on a sheet of greasproof paper. Put another sheet on top and roll meat with a rolling pin to form a neat rectangle, about 10 x 6 inches, of even thickness. Discard the top layer of paper. Mix sweetcorn and chopped mushrooms with rest of the onion mixture. Season well. Lay the stuffing in a neat line on the meat rectangle, about 3 inches from the edge nearest you. Using the under-layer of greaseproof paper to help you, carefully roll up like a swiss roll. Transfer to a foil-lined tin. Mix together the glaze ingredients and paint the roll. Bake for 45 minutes.

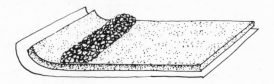 

Stovies

There are different ideas on how stovies should be made. Every cook thinks his or her recipe is the one and only method, and everyone else's is wrong. Some very strange things go into other people's stovies — haggis, liver, mince and even sausages. It can be quite unwise to get involved in an argument on the true nature of stovies. As in politics, people are not really rational about it. In our household, stovies were a Monday dish, made to stretch the tattered remains of the Sunday joint to make a second meal. The meat was chopped fine and stirred through the stovies so that everyone had some of it in his serving. Any gravy or dripping in the meat tin went into the pot as well, for flavour and richness.

potatoes	gravy and dripping
1 onion	meat stock cube, optional
left-over roast meat	

Heat some dripping, or cooked fat from the joint, cut small, in a heavy-base saucepan. When very hot, put in a chopped onion or a few diced shallots, and fry. Peel and slice as many potatoes as you need for the number of servings. Add to the pan with a good shake of salt and pepper. Chop up any scraps remaining from the joint and put into the pot with a spoonful or two of left-over gravy if you have any. If not, add no more than 2 tablespoons of water, and a crumbled meat stock cube. Cover tightly, and cook very gently, without lifting the lid, for 1-2 hours, depending on the amount of potatoes. When ready, scrape it all up from the pan base with a strong spoon. The scrapings at the bottom should be slightly 'burnt'. Stir it round, so that the end result is brown — stovies *ought* to be brown — and season again if needed. Serve with oatcakes, butter and cheese.

(P.S. This is the right method!)

Corned beef hash

A close relative of stovies.

potatoes	corned beef — allow 4 oz per
large onion, finely chopped	serving
margarine	salt and pepper

Boil the potatoes, drain and mash. Melt 1 oz of margarine in a large strong frypan and cook the onion gently till soft but not brown. Add the potatoes and press down to cover the base of the pan. Mash the corned beef and press into the potatoes. Cook gently till a brown crust forms on the underside of the potatoes. Stir it all up to mix the crust through the pan contents. Repeat once or twice, adding a little more margarine to the pan as required, until the mixture is piping hot and crusty. Season generously before serving.

Potted hough

1 lb shin of beef
knuckle bone
bay leaf

salt
20 peppercorns

Wash the meat and bone. Cover with water. Add the flavourings. Bring to the boil, skim, reduce heat to a simmer and cook for 2 hours. Remove the beef and cook the stock for 2 more hours. Cut up meat from the shin and bone and place in small moulds. Strain the stock and pour over the shredded meat. Leave until set. Turn out. Serve with toast or salad.

Scotch pies

Small mutton pies are the favourite Scots snack food, available everywhere — from the hot cupboards of bakers and pubs alike. The makers of the pies take pride in the fine quality of their own product, so that it can be a good everyday food buy. The pies have a rim about half an inch above the lid, and can be filled with hot gravy, potatoes, or peas with a good splash of vinegar as the Glaswegians eat them. Some pies have a piped swirl of creamed potato instead of a lid.

Filling
12 oz lean mutton or lamb
1 small onion, finely chopped
salt and pepper

Worcester sauce
little stock to moisten

Hot water pastry
1 lb plain flour
4 oz dripping
½ pint water

good pinch salt
beaten egg to glaze

Filling Mix the meat with onion and seasonings and stir in a pan over a moderate heat for about 10 minutes to heat through and release the meat juices. Moisten with a little stock. Some bakers add a little breadcrumb to the filling.

Hot water pastry Pre-heat oven to 200°C/400°F/gas mark 6. Melt the fat in the water and bring up to the boil. Sieve the flour and salt in a bowl, make a well in the centre and pour in the liquid. Mix together with the blade of a knife, turn out and knead until the dough is smooth. Cut off a third of the pastry for the lid, slip it into a polythene bag and keep it warm. Roll out the larger piece thinly and line small straight-sided pie tins, or shape the pastry over the base of a jam jar. The cases should be about 1½ inches deep, and 3 inches across the base. Place on a baking sheet. Spoon in the filling. Roll out the pastry for the lids and cut a small hole in the centre. Brush tops with beaten egg. Bake for 45 minutes. Serve hot.   MAKES 6-8

☙☙☙☙☙☙☙☙☙☙☙☙

VENISON

Venison is a lean and tasty meat. Cook it in any of the ways you would use for beef. The tenderness of the flesh depends on the age of the animal, and on the length of time it has been hung. As you will probably have no way of knowing this it is a good idea, when planning a venison dish, to allow enough time beforehand to steep the meat in a marinade for anything from 12 hours to 3 days. After 24 hours any cut of venison will be tender. Only leave it longer than this if you like an increasingly 'gamey' flavour. Even the best roasting cuts benefit from being marinaded. If using a frozen joint, the juices that come from the meat as it thaws mingle with the marinade, and so are not lost, as the strained marinade can often be used as part of the cooking liquid. When you remove the joint from the marinade, do not wash the meat — just pat it dry with kitchen paper, and proceed with your chosen method of cooking.

A marinade contains an acid (lemon juice, vinegar, cider, wine or wine vinegar) to tenderise the fibres of the meat, an oil to keep the meat moist, and flavouring from herbs and spices. A marinade for venison often contains juniper berries. You can find these easily in the spice section of any large supermarket. Bruise them with a rolling pin to release their volatile oils into the marinade. There is never any salt in a marinade, as this would draw out the meat juices, which toughens the meat.

A marinade for venison

¼ pint olive or sunflower oil | a bay leaf
¼ pint red wine (or vinegar, | 4 peppercorns
or wine and vinegar mixed) | 4 juniper berries bruised
1 small onion thinly sliced

Combine the ingredients in a deep dish and turn the venison joint in it to coat. Occasionally turn the joint during the marinading time.

Roast venison

2-3 lb roasting cut of venison | venison marinade (as above)
from the saddle or haunch | port (optional)
butter | salt and pepper
6-10 streaky bacon rashers

Soak the meat in the venison marinade for 24 hours. Lift out, pat dry with kitchen paper. Trim any ragged ends and cut off any deer fat, which is not usually eaten. Rub the joint all over with butter, and wrap it in the bacon rashers to keep it moist. Set a large square of foil over a meat tin, place the joint on the centre and draw the edges of the foil together above the meat, to form a 'tent'. Cook at 190°C/375°F/gas mark 5, allowing 30 minutes per lb and 30 minutes extra. Test for tenderness. Pour off the meat juices to make gravy. Season and add a little port if liked. Have redcurrant or rowan jelly on the table, to serve.

Happit venison

'Wrapped' venison. A recipe from Ballater on Deeside. In the days before the miracle of kitchen foil, venison was roasted in a jacket made with a flour-and-water, or flour-and-suet paste. It is still a very tasty way to serve venison.

2-4 lb roasting cut of venison, marinaded	½ lb suet
	salt and pepper
1 lb SR flour	3 oz butter

Pre-heat the oven to 180°C/350°F/gas mark 4. Choose a meat tin according to the size of your joint. Set the grill rack from your cooker into the tin to hold the meat above the tin base. Make a suet crust for the joint by mixing the flour, suet and seasoning well with enough water to give a rather stiff dough. The amount of crust you need to make depends on the size of the joint. Roll out the crust about ½ inch thick on a floured worktop, keeping the rolling pin well dusted with flour. Sprinkle the meat with seasoned flour and wrap it in the crust, pinching any cracks to make sure that the joint is completely enclosed. Melt the butter in the meat pan and set the wrapped joint on the rack. Roast, allowing 30 minutes to the lb, and basting the crust from time to time. When cooked, switch off the heat, and allow the joint to rest in the oven for half an hour, with the door open. Break open the crust, carve the meat and season the juices remaining in the tin, to serve as a gravy. Serve a piece of the crust with the meat. Have a sharp-flavoured jelly as an accompaniment.

Braised venison

2 lb rolled leg of venison	1 bay leaf
1 oz dripping	6 peppercorns
1 carrot, onion, leek, and stick of celery, diced	6 juniper berries, bruised
	salt and pepper
6 rashers streaky bacon	½ pint stock (beef, chicken or
marinade (see p. 36)	game)

Mix the marinade in a deep dish, turn the venison in it and leave for 24 hours or longer, occasionally turning the meat. Take out the joint and pat dry with kitchen paper. Heat the dripping in a large pan with a sturdy base and brown the meat all over. Take out the meat and put the vegetables in the pan, stirring to coat, cover and allow to cook gently for a few minutes. Meanwhile wrap the venison with the streaky bacon rashers, tucking in the ends to hold in place — use one or two cocktail sticks if necessary. Put the joint on top of the vegetables. Strain the marinade and mix it with the stock and spices. Pour round the venison. Cover the pot, bring to the boil, lower heat to a simmer, and cook for 2 hours. Inspect the pot occasionally to check that the liquid does not need topping up. Test for tenderness. Allow a little longer if necessary. Add salt to the pot only at the end of the cooking time. Serve sliced, still in its bacon jacket, with creamed potatoes and a green vegetable. Strain the gravy, pass a sheet of kitchen paper over the surface to skim the fat, check seasoning, and serve with the meat. Rowan or redcurrant jelly is a pleasant accompaniment.

Venison casserole

1½ lb venison shoulder
2 tablesp flour
2 oz butter
1 large onion, chopped
1 clove garlic, crushed
¼ pint red wine

2 rounded tablesp redcurrant
 jelly
level teasp ground ginger
salt and pepper
meat stock

Pre-heat oven to 180°C/350°F/gas mark 4. Cut the meat into ¾ inch cubes and flour the pieces. Melt the butter in a pan and cook the onion and garlic until soft. Add the floured meat and turn in the butter until lightly browned. Add the wine, redcurrant jelly and ginger and stir thoroughly to scrape up the pan flavourings, then turn into a 2 pint casserole. Add enough meat stock to just cover the meat. Cover the casserole and cook for 2-3 hours until tender. Check the level of the stock during the cooking time. Season. Serve with mashed potatoes and oatcakes. Braised celery accompanies venison well, and can be cooked alongside the casserole towards the end of the cooking time.

Venison curry Venison makes a superb curry. Cook exactly as you would for a beef curry.

Puddings

THE SUMMER fruits of Grampian give a lot of scope to the cook for exciting puddings to end a meal. A clump of everday rhubarb grows in a corner of nearly every garden, a few stalks providing a dish of juicy tart fruit to serve with custard or cream, or in pies and crumbles. In season, strawberries and raspberries with cream or the top-of-the-milk are a daily treat, for these native fruits grow well in the northeast.

In the cold winter days, apple pies and steamed puddings are appreciated, and on Hogmanay a good slice of your host's Clootie Dumpling will give you stamina to see the night through.

Cranachan (cream crowdie)

Many consider this the most delicious Scottish sweet of all. It was a harvest dish, a celebration mixture of cream and oatmeal.

1 rounded tablesp oatmeal
½ pint double cream
2 tablesp rum, or any
   favourite liqueur, sherry,
   wine etc.

2 oz caster sugar
½ lb soft fruit —
   raspberries, strawberries,
   blaeberries, etc.

Toast the oatmeal lightly in the oven or under the grill. Any grade of oatmeal can be used from coarse to fine. Set aside to cool. Whisk the

39

cream, add the sugar, and whisk again until it just holds its shape. Fold in the oatmeal and your preferred flavouring. Chill briefly. Just before serving, pile the soft fruit on the top.

Note The sweet should be chilled for a short time only (i.e. for not more than one hour before serving) so that the oatmeal does not lose its crisp nuttiness.

Blaeberry puffs

In late July the blaeberries are ready on the heather moors in Deeside. The berries are small, so it takes a while to gather enough to use for 4 people. A small cupful is enough for this recipe.

Puffs
2½ oz plain flour	pinch salt
2 eggs, size 3	1 teasp sugar
2 oz butter or hard margarine	¼ pint water

Filling
5 oz carton double or whipping cream	1 tablesp caster sugar
	1 cup blaeberries

Preheat oven to 200°C/400°F/gas mark 6. Sift the flour on to a piece of greaseproof paper. Beat the eggs lightly. Melt the margarine, sugar, salt and water together in a saucepan, and slowly bring to the boil. As soon as the mixture boils, draw the pan from the heat and shoot the flour in all at once. Beat with a wooden spoon or an electric hand whisk. Return to a very low heat and beat for 1 minute until the mixture forms a ball and leaves the sides of the pan clean. Do not over-beat. Draw from the heat. Cool for 2 minutes then beat in eggs gradually. Spoon out the mixture into 8 heaps on a wetted baking sheet. (Steam forms and helps them to rise.) Bake for 20 minutes, then reduce the temperature to 190°C/375°F/gas mark 5 for 15 minutes. Transfer to a cooling rack, and pierce the buns with the point of a knife to release the steam. Split the buns when cold.

To fill the puffs Whip the cream until softly stiff, sweeten with sugar and fold in the blaeberries. Bruise a few of the berries so that the juice runs and marbles the cream. Fill each puff generously.

Note Soft tub margarine is not suitable. Strong bread flour gives crisper results because of a higher gluten content. It is easily obtained at large supermarkets, but ordinary plain flour will give reasonable results. Self-raising flour is never used as the raising agent spoils the buns.

If the oven door is opened during the cooking time, the puffs will collapse.

40

Currant sorbet

Sorbets are water ices whipped to a smooth fluffy texture. A sherbet has cream or yoghurt added to the basic sorbet. They are a light and fresh end to a meal, but some cooks like to serve them between main courses to refresh the palate.

1 lb red or black currants	3 oz sugar
1 tablesp red currant jelly	2 egg whites
2 tablesp lemon juice	

Make a syrup by dissolving the sugar in ¼ pint water. Boil for 5 minutes. Cook the currants and jelly in ¼ pint water with the lemon juice until soft, then puree and sieve the fruit. Mix the pulp with the syrup. Pour into a shallow container and freeze until slushy. Whip the egg whites until stiff. Turn out the fruit mixture into a cold bowl, beat thoroughly to break down the ice crystals, and fold in the egg whites. Return to the container and freeze again until slushy. Beat once more to obtain smooth sorbet. Return to the container. Freeze. Place in the fridge to soften slightly, about half an hour before serving.

Ice bowl For a special occasion, serve the scoops of sorbet in an ice bowl. This remains intact for a long time. To make, two thin light flat-bottomed bowls are required, one at least 2 inches smaller than the other. Place the smaller bowl inside the larger, and pour just enough water into the larger bowl so that the rim of the smaller bowl floats up level with that of the larger. Freeze. To keep the inner bowl in position while freezing, lay a strip of sticky tape across all the rims to hold everything lightly in place. When frozen, check that the smaller bowl is sitting exactly on centre. If not, release it by pouring a little hot water briefly into the smaller bowl, then reposition it and place a weight inside it. Fill the gap between the two bowls with water. Freeze. Remove the two bowls as soon as the mould has frozen, by dipping the outer bowl in hot water, and pouring a little hot water inside the smaller. Keep the ice bowl in the freezer until required. To use, stand on a pretty plate and filled with scoops of sorbet.

Bramble sherbet

1 lb brambles	5 oz carton natural yogurt or
1 tablesp bramble jelly	whipping cream, lightly
2 egg whites	whipped

Sugar syrup

2 oz sugar	¼ pint water
1 tablesp honey	

Cook the brambles with the jelly and ¼ pint water until soft. Push through a sieve. Make a sugar syrup by dissolving the sugar and honey in the water and boil for 5 minutes to concentrate the sugar. Combine the puree, the syrup, and the yogurt or cream. Freeze in a shallow container. Stir several times while it is freezing. When it is slushy in texture, whisk the egg whites until stiff, then fold in. Freeze until solid. Serve in scoops, with shortbread fingers.

Bramble mist

This recipe uses Drambuie (an dram buidheach, 'the drink which pleases'), the whisky liqueur of Prince Charles Edward Stuart. He gave his recipe to the Mackinnons of Strathaird on Skye in return for their shelter and hospitality. The recipe is still a secret of the Mackinnon family, and the essence is prepared before being taken to the factory to be blended into malt whisky.

1 lb very ripe brambles	2 oz caster sugar
2 tablesp Drambuie	½ pint whipping cream

Wash the brambles and keep back a few for decoration. Whisk the cream, sugar and Drambuie until softly thick and fold in the fruit. Spoon into 4 serving glasses. Top with a few brambles and chill lightly before serving.

Rhubarb and date tart

Pastry
8 oz plain flour	4 oz butter or margarine
pinch salt	1 egg
1 oz caster sugar	milk and sugar to glaze

Filling
	1 tablesp lemon juice
3-4 sticks young rhubarb	pinch cinnamon
4 oz chopped dates	
1 tablesp sugar	

Preheat oven to 220°C/425°F/gas mark 7. Stir flour and salt on a board, make a well in the centre and add sugar, butter and the egg. Blend together, gradually drawing the flour into the centre, then form into a ball, put into a polythene bag, and chill for 30 minutes. Roll out on a lightly floured surface, line an 8 inch sandwich tin and lightly prick the base. Chop the rhubarb and scatter over the pastry base with the dates. Sprinkle over the sugar — not too much, as the dates will sweeten the fruit to some extent. Squeeze over the lemon juice and scatter a pinch of cinnamon. Cover with the rest of the pastry. To glaze the top, paint with a little milk and sprinkle with caster sugar. Bake for 30 minutes. Serve with custard or pouring cream.

Bramble and date tart

Make in the same way as for rhubarb tart, substituting 8 oz brambles for rhubarb.

Eve's pudding

1 lb cooking apples
little lemon juice
2 tablesp water
2 tablesp sugar
2 oz margarine

2 oz caster sugar
1 egg
4 oz SR flour
little milk to mix

Preheat oven to 190°C/375°F/gas mark 5. Peel, core and slice the apples and put into a 2 pint pie dish. Sprinkle with lemon juice and add the sugar and water. Cream the sugar and margarine and add the egg gradually with a little of the flour to prevent curdling. Fold in the rest of the flour. Add a little milk, enough to give a soft dropping consistency. Spread the mixture over the apples to cover completely. Bake for 45 minutes.

Apple crumble

apples prepared as in Eve's
pudding recipe
6 oz plain flour
3 oz margarine

2 oz caster sugar
1 tablesp ground ginger or
cinnamon, optional
sprinkling of demerara sugar

Preheat oven to 200°C/400°F/gas mark 6. Stir the spice into the flour. Cut up the margarine and rub lightly into the flour. Mix in the caster sugar. Spoon the mixture over the apples and press it down very gently. Sprinkle with a little demerara sugar. Bake for 45 minutes.

Any other soft fruit can be used for these puddings.

Gooseberry whip

A light summer party sweet.

1½ lb gooseberries
3 oz sugar
3 egg yolks
3 oz caster sugar
1 envelope gelatine

1 or 2 drops green colouring
(optional)
3 egg whites
¼ pint double cream
crystallised rose petals

Top and tail gooseberries, rinse and simmer them gently with the sugar and 3 tablespoons water until soft. Push them through a sieve. Beat the egg yolks and caster sugar together until thick and pale. Stir in the puree. Cook gently over a bowl of hot (not boiling) water as if making a curd, until the mixture thickens. Melt gelatine in a little lukewarm water in an old cup standing in a saucepan of hot water. Stir it through the fruit mixture. Tint with one or two drops of green colouring. Chill. Whisk egg whites till stiff, fold into the cold mixture. Pour into individual glasses. Whip the cream and swirl it over the mixture in each glass to cover. Decorate with crystallised rose petals.

Grampian pears

A glorious autumn sweet.

4 pears	1 oz soft brown sugar
4 tablesp whisky	1 oz fine oatmeal
1 oz butter	¼ pint whipping cream

Preheat oven to 190°C/375°F/gas mark 5. Peel and slice the pears, and place in a shallow oven dish. Spoon over the whisky, allowing one tablespoon per pear. Cover the dish and bake for half an hour in the middle shelf. If the pears are hard, they may take a little longer. Meanwhile, mash the butter, sugar and oatmeal together and spread thinly on a baking sheet. Bake for 15 minutes, on a lower shelf. Remove from oven, and either curl round a wooden handle as for brandy snaps, while still warm, or allow to cool, then crumble. Divide the pears and juice between 4 individual serving dishes. Whip the cream till softly stiff then spread over the pears. Sprinkle over the oat crumb or place a curled oat snap in the cream. Serve while the pears are still slightly warm.

Note The rich home-made ice cream (p. 47) can be used instead of cream.

Party meringues

Crisp outside, soft marshmallow inside, everyone loves these!
Makes 12.

4 egg whites (size 2)	9 oz caster sugar
1 teasp vanilla essence	1 teasp vinegar

Set the oven at 150°C/300°F/gas mark 2. Line 2 swiss roll tins with non-stick baking parchment. Put the egg whites into a large bowl and whip with an electric whisk until very thick and standing up in stiff peaks. Gradually add the sugar, about 2 tablespoons at a time, continuing to whisk so that the meringue is thick and glossy. Finally whisk in the vanilla essence (real essence, not vanilla flavouring) and vinegar. Spoon out the meringue into 12 heaps. Swirl the top of each meringue into a neat circle and slightly hollow out the centre. Use the centre and lower shelves of the oven and bake for 15 minutes, then change over the position of the trays. Lower the temperature to 100°C/200°F/gas mark ¼ for 45 minutes — watch that the meringues do not start to colour — then switch off the oven and leave till cold, or overnight. To serve, fill the centres with softly whisked whipping cream, and top with a sliced strawberry, a few rasps or fruit in season. The meringues store well in an airtight tin.

Strawberry syllabub

½ lb strawberries   ¼ pint white wine
½ pint whipping cream   2 teasp lemon juice
2 tablesp runny honey

Divide the strawberries between 4 glasses, keeping back 4 for decoration. Put the cream, honey, wine and lemon juice in a bowl and whisk till the mixture forms soft peaks. Spoon into the glasses. Chill until required. To serve, top with the reserved fruit.

Orange and lemon cheesecake

I serve this lovely cheesecake, light, tangy and not too sweet, on special occasions, and at Christmas as an alternative sweet.

Base
6 oz digestive biscuits   2 level tablesp cocoa
2 level tablesp syrup   2 oz butter

Topping
2 oranges   4 oz caster sugar
1 lemon   1 lb cottage cheese
¾ oz gelatine   5-oz carton whipping cream

To make base   Crush biscuits in a processor, or put into a polythene bag and crush with a rolling pin. Melt butter, cocoa and syrup in a saucepan over a gentle heat, then stir in the crumbs. Spread the biscuit mixture on the base of an 8-inch loose-based cake tin, minimum 2½ inches deep. Level the surface with the back of a spoon. Press down very lightly.

To make topping   Wash and dry the oranges and lemon. Put 3 tablespoons cold water into a Pyrex measuring jug and sprinkle on the gelatine. Stand the jug in a pan of hot water, off the heat, until the gelatine melts. Lightly grate the fruits to obtain fine shreds of the rind (avoid the pith). Halve the fruit and squeeze out the juice. Add juice and shreds of rind to the jug. Add a little cold water, if necessary, to make up to half a pint. Stir in the sugar until dissolved. Put the cottage cheese into a liquidiser, with some of the fruit syrup. Spin until smooth, gradually adding the rest of the fruit syrup. Pour the mixture into a large bowl. Whip the cream to soft thickness, then stir into the cheese mixture. Pour over the biscuit base. Allow to set in the fridge.

To serve   Decorate with chocolate leaves (page 83) — I use holly leaves at Christmas — or small crystallised orange and lemon jelly sweets.

45

Fruit cream

An old-fashioned favourite

½ pint fruit, pureed and
   sieved
¼ pint unsweetened custard
¼ pint double cream
1 packet gelatine (½ oz)

2 oz caster sugar
few drops almond essence
2 teasp lemon juice
2 drops edible colouring, if
   needed

Mix the fruit puree, sugar, custard, almond essence and lemon juice together. Whip the cream lightly and fold into the mixture. Tint with the colouring if necessary. Dissolve the gelatine in a little lukewarm water in an old cup standing in a bowl of hot water. Stir the melted gelatine into the fruit mixture. Pour into a glass bowl and leave until set. If liked, decorate with a few chopped nuts or some chocolate leaves (p. 83).

Note Strawberries and raspberries can be sieved and used fresh. Most fruits will need to be cooked before pureeing.

Brown-top gooseberry plate pie

Use the first gooseberries of summer in this delicious tart. Good with young pink rhubarb too.

Pastry
6 oz plain flour
1½ oz lard

1½ oz margarine
cold water to mix

Filling
8 oz gooseberries
1 egg
1 teasp ground cinnamon

3 oz caster sugar
1 teasp cornflour
1 oz SR flour

To make the pastry Preheat the oven to 190°C/375°F/gas mark 5. Cut the fats into small pieces and rub lightly into the flour till you have the texture of fine breadcrumbs. Add about 2 tablespoons cold water and mix with a fork to make a firm dough. Roll out to 9 inches diameter and lay on a lightly oiled 8-inch oven-proof plate, the pastry hanging 1 inch over the edge. Fold back the overlap, and pinch it into a rim wall all round the edge of the plate.

To make the filling Top, tail and wash the gooseberries. Mix the cornflour with 1 oz of the caster sugar, and stir into the berries. Spread over the pastry. Put the remaining 2 oz of sugar and the egg into a bowl and beat with an electric hand whisk until thick. Sift the flour and cinnamon together and fold into the mixture. Spread over the berries. Bake about an hour until golden, and dust with fine sugar. Serve hot or cold, on its own or with whipped cream or thick Greek yogurt.

Ice cream

The northeaster will make short work of a cappie or slider (cone or wafer) on a hot summer day. This easy one-stage velvety ice cream uses the modern meringue method.

3 eggs, size 3
2 rounded tablesp caster
    sugar
1 packet dessert topping mix   (for everyday)
    OR
6 oz carton whipping cream   (for a special occasion)
    (fresh or UHT)
few drops vanilla essence

Whip the cream and essence until softly thick, or make up the dessert topping mix with milk according to the packet directions. Separate the eggs. Whisk the whites until very stiff, then beat in the sugar gradually to obtain a thick shiny meringue. Mix in the egg yolks lightly, so as not to knock out the air. Fold in the cream or topping mix. Pour into a lidded plastic 2 litre box and freeze.

Note If you have a grinder, reduce the sugar to icing sugar texture, to give the ice cream extra smoothness. Commercial icing sugar is not suitable for the recipe, because the preservative leaves a noticeable flavour.

Serving variations

Add 1 cup of crushed raspberries, stirred in lightly to marble the ice cream, before freezing.

For a party sweet, add a cup of crushed raspberries and a few drops of almond essence to the mixture before freezing. Serve with shortbread fingers.

Add 1 tablespoon lightly toasted oatmeal to the basic ice cream before freezing.

Serve as **Baked Alaska**. Place a plain sponge round on an ovenproof plate. Sprinkle it with 3 tablespoons sherry. Whisk 3 egg whites until very stiff and beat in 4 oz caster sugar to make a shiny meringue. Place the frozen block of ice cream (with raspberries) on the sponge. Completely cover with the meringue. Bake in a preheated oven(230⁰ C/450⁰F/gas mark 8) for no more than 4 minutes. Remove from oven, and serve immediately, if possible. If properly insulated by the meringue, the ice cream will stay firm for a short while before serving.

Clafouti

A French cherry recipe. In France, the dish would be made using red or black cherries, but you can experiment with any soft fruit, and it is especially delicious made with Scottish raspberries.

1 oz butter
2 eggs
2 oz caster sugar
2 oz plain flour
1 tablesp melted butter
¼ pint milk

1 tablesp rum or brandy
(optional)
pinch salt
½ lb cherries, raspberries. or
fruit of your choice

Preheat oven to 220°C/425°F/gas mark 7. Rub ½ oz of the butter over a shallow oven dish. Whisk the eggs lightly in a bowl, blend in the flour sifted with the salt, then mix in the sugar. Heat the milk gently to lukewarm, stir in the rum or brandy if using, and whisk into the mixture with the melted butter. Pour a little of the batter into the dish, just enough to cover the bottom, and bake for 5 minutes only, until the mixture is just set. Scatter the fruit over the surface and pour in the rest of the batter. Flake the remaining ½ oz of butter over the top. Bake for 25 minutes. Allow to cool for a while before cutting, and serve just warm, with cream or ice cream. Left-over clafouti can be cut into small squares and eaten cold.

Pumpkin pie

An American speciality for Thanksgiving Day celebrations (the fourth Tuesday of November), first held in 1621 by the Plymouth colony on the occasion of their first harvest.

Pastry
6 oz plain flour
pinch salt
1½ oz margarine

1½ oz lard
1 oz caster sugar or soft
brown sugar

Filling
1 lb slice pumpkin
1 oz butter
2 eggs
¼ pint single cream
2 oz soft brown sugar

1 teasp ground cinnamon
1 teasp ground ginger
¼ teasp ground nutmeg
2 tablesp brandy (optional)

whipped cream, to serve

Preheat oven to 200°C/400°F/gas mark 6. To make the pastry, stir the flour with the salt and sugar, then rub in the fats until like fine breadcrumbs. Bind the mixture with about 2 tablespoons water and roll out. Line an 8 or 9 inch flan dish or pie plate. Chill in the fridge while you make the filling. Skin the pumpkin, cut into 1 inch pieces and put in a saucepan with the butter. Cover and cook gently until soft. A lot of liquid comes from the pumpkin as it softens, so, towards the end of the cooking time, remove the lid and raise the heat slightly to evaporate some of the excess liquid. Puree the pumpkin and allow to cool. Beat together the eggs, cream, sugar, spices and brandy (if using), then add the pumpkin puree. Pour into the prepared pie case. Bake for 40 minutes. Allow to cool. Serve with a bowl of whipped cream dusted with nutmeg.

TRADITIONAL SPECIALITIES

Yirned milk (curds, junket)

Yirned milk — curds and whey — is fresh milk clotted with rennet, a gentle fermenting agent which converts milk sugar into lactic acid. Originally of animal origin, rennet is now sold in liquid or tablet form, but tends to lose its strength if stored too long. It is also possible to make curds and whey with buttermilk, using two parts buttermilk to fresh milk, the texture being slightly softer. Junket is a dish of sweetened curds.

1 pint milk	1 tablesp brandy (optional)
1 teasp sugar	cream
1 teasp rennet	pinch nutmeg or cinnamon

Bring milk with sugar to blood heat. Test with your (clean) little finger. Set out 2 or 3 individual glass dishes or 1 large bowl and spoon in the brandy. Stir in the warm milk. Lastly add the rennet. Cover and leave at room temperature until set (about an hour). It must not be put into the fridge until it is set. Do not disturb or cut it, or it will separate into curds and whey. For this reason it is better to make it up in individual servings. Chill before eating.

To serve Pour a little cream gently over the surface to coat. Sprinkle with a pinch of nutmeg or cinnamon.

Note It is important not to warm the milk above blood heat or the curds will not set.

Crowdie

2 pints milk   1 teasp rennet

Make up a plain junket using the method described on page 49. After the curd has set, disturb it by cutting and chopping in the bowl. The curd will separate from the whey, which will rise to the top. Leave it for a while in a warm place, then line a colander with a piece of cheesecloth or muslin and turn the whole dish into the colander to drain for an hour or two (the whey can be used instead of fat for making oatcakes). Then break up the curds with the fingers, and salt lightly. Serve in small individual bowls. Eat with oatcakes and butter.

Crowdie-and-cream

Mix a tablespoon of thick cream into the salted crowdie. Form into a pat and serve with oatcakes and butter, on its own or as an alternative to a sweet. Each serving should have approximately 2 parts of crowdie to 1 of cream.

Oatcakes

8 oz oatmeal   pinch baking soda
½ teasp salt   boiling water to mix
1 tablesp melted fat

Mix the dry ingredients. Make a well in the centre, put in the fat and mix with boiling water to a stiff dough. Turn out on to a surface generously dusted with oatmeal. Knead and roll out thinly with hands well floured with oatmeal. Rub the dough with the meal to keep it white. Using an inverted dinner plate, press out two rounds, then cut into quarters. Bake the oatcakes for half an hour in a moderate oven (180°C/ 350°F/gas mark 4), if you are not using a girdle.

Athole brose cream

4 oz medium oatmeal   2 tablesp runny heather honey
½ pint cold water   ¼ pint whipping cream
¼ pint whisky

Soak the oatmeal in the water and allow to stand for an hour. Push through a fine sieve, pressing to obtain the milky fluid. Discard the oatmeal. Mix the oatmeal extract with the honey, whisky and cream. Serve in small glasses. If preferred, prepare the brose but whip the cream separately, and serve topped with the whipped cream and a sprinkling of toasted oatmeal.

Clootie dumpling

A basin can be used instead of the cloot if preferred, but the pudding will not have the characteristic skin. Small charms or coins wrapped in greaseproof paper can be added for a special celebration.

6 oz SR flour	1 teasp cinnamon
extra pinch baking powder	pinch nutmeg
4 oz breadcrumbs	8 oz mixed sultanas/currants
2 oz oatmeal	1 tablesp syrup
4 oz shredded suet	1 tablesp treacle
4 oz soft brown sugar	few tablesp buttermilk or
1 egg	sweet milk, to mix
2 teasp ground ginger	

Dip the cloot (a piece of cotton or linen roughly a yard square) in boiling water, then wring it, open out and dredge with flour. Lay it across a bowl, to support the pudding while filling the cloot. Stir all the dry ingredients together in another bowl, make a well in the centre, and mix in the treacle, syrup, egg and enough buttermilk or milk to give a fairly soft but firm texture. Spoon into the cloot. Gather up the cloot and tie the ends tightly with string but allowing a space for the pudding to swell. Stand the dumpling on a plate on the base of a saucepan, and fill up with boiling water to cover. Cover the pan and simmer for 2-3 hours. Remove the dumpling into a colander. Open up the cloot, peeling it back carefully from the dumpling. Put a plate over the colander and quickly turn it over. Carefully pull the cloot away from the dumpling. There is no need to dry off the pudding. Dredge with fine sugar. Serve hot with custard, or eat cold like a cake. Leftover dumpling can be used for other meals:

 fry slices in hot butter. Serve sprinkled with caster sugar and cream.

 fry slices in hot butter and serve with bacon.

wrap slices in foil and heat in the oven. Serve with cream.

Flycups & Pieces

EARLY IN THE century, a Scottish dialect dictionary gave the fly cup respectability, defining it as 'a quick cup of tea, taken as a refresher between meals', but the term very probably originated in the notion of a surreptitious cup of tea snatched at a time when tea drinking was less common. Tea was a luxury, taken only at arranged times in the afternoon and evening. Nevertheless, even today, the delicious hint of guilt surrounding the little ceremony makes it all the more enjoyable.

Along with your fly cup, you will probably have a tasty titbit — a 'piece' as it is called in the Northeast. If it is exceptionally tasty you will refer to it enthusiastically as a 'fine piece'. A piece can be either savoury or sweet.

Northeast housewives are proud of their skill in home-baking and the bakeries have a tempting array of pieces to choose from. Some of the best-loved pieces, however, are slowly disappearing, either because of the high cost of the ingredients or the time cost for hand work in making them. Jap cakes, made from expensive ground almonds, are rarely seen now, likewise sair heidies — soft sponge cakes with paper jackets. A batch made at home is now the only way to taste some of these familiar old pieces, and this section contains some of these recipes.

You can very easily do without your fly cup and your fine piece. In fact, doctors are at pains to tell you that it would be very good for you to do without them. But do you want to?

Butteries

Butteries are not the easiest item to make at home. Professional bakers put the rolls through a steaming process before baking them, and a way has to be found to imitate this, to give the rolls the necessary humidity to help them rise properly. In this recipe, I am using easy-blend yeast, which is stirred directly into the flour before the liquid is added. The main portion of the fat is added by spreading on to the dough as if buttering a slice of bread. It should not be added in pieces as if making flaky pastry.

8 oz strong bread flour	1 slightly rounded teasp
1 teasp salt	easy-blend dried yeast
3 oz butter	¼ pint tepid water
1 oz lard	

Rub 1 oz butter into the flour and salt. Stir in the yeast then add the water and mix to blend thoroughly. Turn out on to a floured surface and knead well. Put the dough inside a lightly oiled polythene bag and leave to rise for 1 hour, in a warm place. Mash the rest of the butter with the lard and a sprinkle of flour. Knead the dough again on a floured surface. Roll out to an oblong about ¼ inch thick. Spread the fat over the dough to within ½ inch of the edges. Fold a third of the dough from the left, into the centre, then from the right, to form a long rectangle. With the edge of a spatula, make chopping motions all along the dough, without breaking through to expose the fat, to incorporate the fat into the dough. Cut the dough into 8 pieces. Form into ovals, turning the corners up and into the centre. Toss in flour, and set them on a floured baking sheet. Knead the tops very gently. Put the tray inside a large polythene bag (a carrier bag is ideal, or a bin liner) and leave to rise for half an hour. If preferred, the rolls can at this point be put into the fridge overnight, but allow to come to room temperature before baking in the morning. Preheat the oven to 200°C/400°F/gas mark 6. Put a roasting tin or the grill pan on the floor of the oven and half-fill it with boiling water. Dust the rolls lightly with salted flour and place the tray near the top of the oven. Bake for 20 minutes, then remove the tin of water and bake for 10 minutes more to brown the butteries. Eat hot. It is better to make the rolls in small batches for immediate use. Multiply the ingredient amounts for a larger batch. The rolls freeze well, and should be toasted to reheat before eating. MAKES 8

Cream scones

8 oz SR flour
pinch salt
1 oz margarine

1 egg
¼ pint sour cream

Preheat oven to 220°C/425°F/gas mark 7. Sieve the flour and the salt. Rub in the margarine. Make a well in the centre and pour in the egg and cream beaten together. Mix from the centre, gradually working in the flour. Turn out, and knead lightly. Roll into a square ¾ inch thick. Cut into triangles. Bake for about 10 minutes.

Cream can be soured by the addition of a little lemon juice.

Treacle scones

8 oz plain flour
½ teasp salt
½ teasp bicarbonate of soda
½ teasp cream of tartar
2 oz margarine

1 teasp mixed spice
1 tablesp caster sugar
1 tablesp molasses or treacle
milk or buttermilk to mix

Preheat oven to 220°C/425°F/gas mark 7. Rub the margarine into the flour until like breadcrumbs. Mix all the dry ingredients, and stir in. Melt the treacle with a little milk or buttermilk and mix in to obtain a stiff dough. Turn on to a floured surface and form into a square about ¾ inch thick. Press mixture gently together, until crack-free, but avoid over-handling. Cut into squares or triangles. Bake 10-15 minutes.

Note The buttermilk makes very light scones.

Sunflower seed oaties

A nutty, crunchy, any-time biscuit. Makes 24.

4 oz sunflower margarine
3 teasp hot water
5 oz SR flour
1 oz sunflower seeds

3 oz granulated sugar
1 teasp treacle
2 oz rolled oats

Mix the margarine and sugar together by hand or in a processor. Add the hot water then the treacle which will slip easily from the hot wet spoon. Beat together. Work in the flour, oats and sunflower seeds. Roll mixture into 24 walnut-size balls and place on a lightly oiled baking sheet. They spread a little on baking. Bake on the middle shelf at 180°C/350°F/gas mark 4 for about 20 minutes till golden. Turn off oven and leave till cold.

Aberdeen crullas

A sweet fried cake, delicious and fragile. They are a speciality of Aberdeen, and were mentioned by Mrs Dalgairns in her Practice of Cookery in 1829. The name has a possible derivation from the Dutch krullen, to curl. In the United States, krullers are similar, and also thought to be of Dutch origin. The northeast fishing community had a longstanding connection with the Dutch fish curers who came to the northeast to impart their skills.

8 oz SR flour
pinch salt
½ teasp ground ginger
2 oz butter
2 oz caster sugar
1 egg

1 tablesp buttermilk (or yogurt, or milk soured with a few drops of lemon juice)
oil for frying
icing sugar

Mix the flour, salt and ginger. Cream the butter and sugar until fluffy. Beat in the egg with a little of the flour to prevent curdling. Stir in the rest of the flour and the buttermilk to obtain a fairly stiff dough. Roll out thinly on a floured surface to a square of approximately 12 inches. Mark into 12 pieces about 4 x 3 inches. Separate. Cut each rectangle into 3 one-inch strips, leaving one end of the rectangle uncut. Fold the outside strips over the centre strip as in a plait. Pinch the open end together to seal. Fry in hot oil to brown, turning once. Dredge with icing sugar and eat hot or cold.

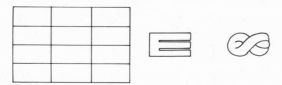

Shortbread

A quick and easy three-flour shortbread, baked in a swiss roll tin.

8 oz plain flour
2 oz corn flour
2 oz rice flour
pinch salt

3 oz butter or rich soft sunflower margarine
4 oz caster sugar

Mix all the ingredients into a smooth paste with a fork, or in a processor. If using butter, it should be softened to room temperature. Put the mixture into a lightly oiled swiss roll tin, pressing out evenly with the back of a fork. Prick lightly all over. Bake at 180°C/350°F/gas mark 4 for 15-20 minutes until pale golden. Mark into fingers or squares, and sprinkle with caster sugar. Return to the oven, switch off the heat and leave until cold.

Cheesecakes

These little sponge cakes are so named because originally the cake mixture was made with a rennet cheese. Although not in the tradition, many people like to find a spot of jam underneath the sponge.

a 12-patty tray lined with flaky or short-crust pastry
4 oz SR flour   1 egg, size 3
2 oz margarine   jam
3 oz caster sugar

Preheat oven to 200°C/400°F/gas mark 6. Put a little jam, if liked, into each of the pastry-lined patty tins. Cream the margarine and sugar and beat in the egg. Fold in the flour. If the mixture is rather stiff, add a teaspoon of milk. Put generous spoonfuls into each patty case. Use any scraps of left-over pastry to make crosses for the top of the cakes and set in position. Bake 20 minutes.

Empire biscuits

Often referred to as 'iced double shortbreads'. The recipe dates from the time when we were encouraged to use the produce of the British Empire. The recipe would have been made with Empire butter.

10 oz SR flour   4 oz icing sugar
4 oz butter or margarine   1 dessertsp lemon juice
3 oz caster sugar   jam
1 teasp cinnamon   glacé cherries or jellied
1 egg   sweets, to decorate

Preheat oven to 190°C/375°F/gas mark 5. Stir the flour and cinnamon together. Beat the butter or margarine and sugar to cream, add the egg, then the flour. Turn out on a floured surface, knead till smooth and roll out ¼ inch thick. Cut into rounds and bake 20 minutes. When cool, cover half the biscuits with jam or jelly and the other half with icing. Put the iced biscuits on top of those with jam. Decorate with a piece of glacé cherry or a sugared ju-jube from a packet of childrens' sweets.

Icing Mix 1 dessertspoon lemon juice into 4 oz icing sugar. Add up to 1 dessertspoon water, a little at a time, until the right consistency is reached.

Variation Before baking, cut a small circle from half of the rounds. After sandwiching the biscuits with jam, brush the tops with melted jam and coat with coconut, leaving the centres clear.   MAKES 17

☙☙☙☙☙☙☙☙☙☙☙☙☙

Gamrie knotties

A kind of sugar-coated rock cake, from Gamrie near Banff, adapted from Hotch Potch *(1951), a collection of recipes from the northeast WI, with a foreword by Priscilla, Lady Tweedsmuir.*

1 lb plain flour	4 oz lard
1 teasp bicarbonate of soda	3 oz caster sugar
1 teasp ground ginger	3 tablesp syrup
1 teasp mixed spice	¼ pint lukewarm milk

Coating
8 oz granulated sugar

Preheat oven to 180°C/350°F/gas mark 4. Stir the flour, soda and spices together, and rub in the lard. Melt the sugar and syrup in the milk over a very low heat. Add to the dry ingredients and mix to a firm dough. Break into pieces and set on a greased tray like rock cakes. Bake 20-30 minutes until golden brown. Cool on a rack. For the coating, melt the sugar slowly over a low heat in 4 tablespoons water, stirring to dissolve. Bring slowly up to the boil and boil for 3 minutes. Allow to cool slightly. Using a skewer to hold the cakes, and working very quickly, dip each one in the syrup. Drain on a rack with a paper set underneath to catch the surplus syrup. The sugar will crystallise on the cakes. Store in a tin.

MAKES 30

Scottish snowballs

8 oz SR flour	8 oz icing sugar
3 oz margarine	2-3 oz desiccated coconut
3 oz caster sugar	pinch salt
1 egg + 1 egg yolk	

Preheat oven to 200°C/400°F/gas mark 6. Stir the flour, sugar and salt together. Rub in the margarine and mix to a stiff dough with the egg and egg yolk. Turn on to a work surface, press into a flat cake, cut into quarters and divide each quarter into 5 pieces — this helps to keep them an even size. Roll each piece into a ball and set the 20 pieces on a greased baking tray. Bake for 15 minutes, and allow to cool. Sandwich the cakes in pairs using a stiff icing made by adding 1 dessertspoon water to 4 oz of icing sugar. Make a thinner coating icing by adding 3 dessertspoons water to the remaining 4 oz icing sugar. Dip the cakes in the icing, removing the excess with a pastry brush, and roll in the desiccated coconut. Leave the icing to set.

Note A bun-tray is useful for holding the snowballs while the icing is setting.

MAKES 10

Sair heidies

'Sore heads' (reform cakes). These well-loved, old-fashioned pieces have all but disappeared from Grampian bakeries. They are straight-sided soft plain sponge cakes wrapped in paper jackets ('bandages' for the sair heid), and have domed heads crusted with lump sugar. They are baked in hand-lined individual rings set on a baking sheet. Possibly the best improvisation for the rings is a set of good-quality metal pastry cutters of the kind that I am using in this recipe. If you like these cakes, you might consider it worthwhile to build up a set. The cutters (2 inches diameter x 1½ inches deep, from good kitchen accessory shops) are versatile items for the cook, as they can also be used as small pie moulds for meats and fruit.

5 oz SR flour	2 eggs
2 oz soft margarine	crushed lump sugar
2 oz caster sugar	

Preheat oven to 200°C/400°F/gas mark 6. Cut 10 paper jackets 6½ inches x 1¾ inches, using either greaseproof paper or ordinary white writing or typing paper, which makes an excellent firm jacket. Working on the baking tray, brush both sides of the jackets with cooking oil. Set the rings on the tray — it is not necessary to grease them — and line the inside of each one with a paper jacket, overlapping the ends about ½ inch. The paper will stand just a little way above the top edge of the rings.

Put the flour, margarine, caster sugar and eggs in a bowl and whisk together thoroughly. Using a teaspoon, divide the mixture evenly between the 10 rings, filling up to about ½ inch from the top edge of the jackets. There is no need to push the mixture down into the moulds as the cakes will fill out the rings as they bake. Sprinkle the top of each cake with a little crushed lump sugar. Bake for 15 minutes. Allow to cool for a minute; you will then be able to push the cakes out of the rings with a little gentle pressure from underneath. Set on a cake rack to cool completely.   MAKES 10

Macaroon tarts

Pastry

3 oz flour
1½ oz margarine
pinch salt

2 teasp cold water
jam (optional)

Filling

2 oz ground almonds
2 oz caster sugar
2 egg whites

little lemon juice or almond essence

Preheat oven to 180°C/350°F/gas mark 4. Rub flour, salt and margarine to fine crumbs, bind with water, roll out and line a 12 hole patty tin. Mix the almonds, juice and sugar and bind with whipped white of egg. If using, put a little jam on the pastry, then half-fill the cases with the almond mixture. Bake for 20 minutes.

Alternative filling A less expensive filling can be made by using desiccated coconut instead of ground almonds.

Fruit cake

An easy, moist, rich cake. I use 32 oz dried fruit and nuts, often varying the combination, eg, to 1 lb standard dried fruit mix, I might add 2 oz each of chopped dried pears, figs, dates, stoned prunes, apricots, coloured glacé cherries, walnuts, mixed peel. This is my Christmas, birthday, all-occasion, foolproof celebration cake!

10 oz plain flour
1 level teasp salt
1 level teasp mixed spice
8 oz soft brown sugar
8 oz soft butter or rich
    sunflower margarine

4 large eggs
1 tablesp black treacle
1 teasp vanilla essence
3 tablesp brandy
32 oz dried fruit and nuts in
    any combination

Sift flour with the spice and salt. Put all the fruits and nuts into a large bowl. Add a rounded tablespoon of the flour. Mix with your hands, to dust and separate the pieces. In a small bowl, beat together the eggs, vanilla and brandy. In your mixing bowl, cream the butter and sugar, then gradually beat in the egg mixture, alternating with a little flour, to avoid curdling (which knocks the air out of the cake). Fold in the flour then the fruit and nuts. Spoon into an 8 inch loose-base deep cake tin, greased and lined base and sides with baking parchment. Hollow the centre a little, then tie or staple a double collar of brown paper round the tin, reaching about 2 inches above the rim. Bake in centre of the oven for 1½ hours at 180°C/350°F/gas mark 4, then 2½ hours at 140°C/275°F/gas mark 1. Test cake with a skewer. Allow to cool for an hour before easing out of the tin.

While the cake is maturing before decoration, 'feed' it a few times with sherry or brandy, piercing with a skewer to let the liquid be inserted.

Coburg cakes

A spicy old favourite. Should not be made too small, and ideally should be made in fluted metal patty tins, but paper cases will do.

6 oz plain flour
pinch salt
scant ½ teasp bicarb of soda
1 teasp mixed spice
1 teasp ground ginger
1 teasp cinnamon
½ teasp nutmeg

3 oz margarine
3 oz caster sugar
1 tablesp treacle
1 egg
little boiling water
few almonds

Pre-heat oven to 180°C/350°F/gas mark 4. Cream the margarine and the sugar, and beat in the treacle. Beat in the egg gradually, with a little bit of the flour if it tends to curdle. Mix the flour with the soda and spices. Beat into the creamed mixture. Put a piece of almond into each paper case, then spoon in the mixture, putting a generous amount in each case. Bake for 25-30 minutes. MAKES 12

Sponge sandwich

A light soft sponge cake made by the easy all-in-one method. Self-raising flour is always used for this type of cake, as it has a correct proportion of baking powder. Because you are not beating in air in the conventional way, extra raising agent has to be added — 1 teaspoon of baking powder for every 4 oz of self-raising flour used. For extra lightness, try the new 'special sponge flour' appearing on supermarket shelves, which can be used for scones also.

4 oz SR or special sponge
    flour
1 level teasp baking powder

4 oz margarine
4 oz caster sugar
2 eggs

Pre-heat oven to 180°C/350°F/gas mark 4. Line two 8-inch sandwich tins (or a single deep tin) and brush with oil. If liked, dust inside with a mixture of 1 teaspoon each of caster sugar and rice flour, to give a crisp cake crust. Sift the flour and baking powder into a bowl, and the sugar, margarine and eggs and beat together with a wooden spoon or electric hand whisk for 2-3 minutes. Put the mixture in the tins, level the top and bake for 25-35 minutes. Cool on a rack. When cold, sandwich with jam and whipped cream or dessert topping mix made up with slightly less milk, to give a stiffer spreading consistency. A butter icing with some lemon curd whipped in gives a filling with a pleasant tartness.

Chocolate sponge Add 1-2 tablespoons cocoa powder, and remove an equal volume of flour to compensate, before starting to make the cake. Try a filling of lime curd and a layer of whipped dessert topping.

Coffee sponge Add 2 oz chopped walnuts or hazelnuts to the flour. Beat in 1-2 tablespoons coffee essence.

60

Scotch perkins

4 oz plain flour
4 oz medium oatmeal
½ teasp bicarbonate of soda
pinch salt
2 oz caster sugar
1 teasp ground ginger

½ teasp cinnamon
½ teasp mixed spice
3 oz lard
1 tablesp treacle
1 tablesp syrup

Pre-heat oven to 180°C/350°F/gas mark 4. Brush a baking sheet with oil. Melt the lard, treacle and syrup together. With a fork, stir all the dry ingredients together. Add the melted mixture and mix well. Roll into balls with your hands and set them on the baking tray. Bake for 20 minutes. The biscuits crispen as they cool. MAKES APPROX 15

Mannies and horses

This is a recipe from the village of Insch, and dates from 1880. The cakes could be bought on market days until the war. They were cut in the shapes of mannies and horses, at first by hand, and later by cutters. (Adapted from Hotch Potch, *1951.)*

8 oz plain flour
¾ teasp bicarbonate of soda
1 teasp ground ginger

3 oz lard
5 tablesp syrup
little warm water, if needed

Pre-heat the oven to 180°C/350°F/gas mark 4. Beat the lard and syrup together. Mix the dry ingredients, and work into the syrup mixture. Roll out and shape into mannies and horses. Bake until golden brown.

The carton cake

This cake has become something of a favourite in the northeast since it was demonstrated on Grampian ITV in August 1983. In the programme it was shown that it can be put together, and the oven door closed on it in just 4 minutes! The carton used is the 5 or 6 fluid oz size.

1 carton hazelnut yogurt
1 carton corn oil
2 cartons caster sugar
3 eggs
pinch salt

3 cartons SR flour
500 g (1.1 lb) packet dried fruit
few chopped nuts and glacé cherries (optional)

Pre-heat oven to 180°C/350°F/gas mark 4. Break the eggs into a bowl with the salt. Add the carton of yogurt. Using the empty carton as your measure, add the corn oil and sugar. Beat together, then stir in the fruit, nuts and cherries. (If you have time, soak the fruit overnight in 1 tablespoon each of orange juice and sherry, to plump the fruit.) Add the flour and beat again. Pour into a greased and base-lined 8 inch loose-bottomed cake tin. Bake for 2 hours, covering the cake with a piece of foil after 1 hour, to prevent over-browning.

Bride slices

Pastry
6 oz flour
4 oz margarine

2 oz caster sugar

Topping
6 oz margarine
6 oz caster sugar
3 eggs
2 tablesp hot water
2 tablesp marmalade

2 tablesp treacle
2 tablesp sherry
1 lb mixed dried fruit
6 oz plain flour
6 oz SR flour

Pre-heat oven to 180°C/350°F/gas mark 4. Rub the margarine into the flour, stir in the sugar, press into a swiss roll tin, and bake for 10 minutes. Cream the margarine and sugar. Beat in the eggs one at a time. Whip in the water, marmalade, treacle and sherry. Add the flour gradually, with the fruit. Spread over the pastry. Bake for 40 minutes.

The cake can be topped with marzipan and icing, if wished, before slicing into fingers.

Fruit slices — 'Flea Cemeteries'

Filling
6 oz mixed raisins and
    currants
1 small apple, peeled and
    cored

1 teasp mixed spice
2 oz soft brown sugar
2 tablesp water
1 level dessertsp flour

Pastry
8 oz SR flour
4 oz margarine

pinch salt
1 egg

Pre-heat oven to 180°C/350°F/gas mark 4. Prepare filling. Grate the apple coarsely and add to the dried fruit. Put all the filling ingredients in a saucepan and heat to the boil, stirring to dissolve the sugar and mix all together. Set aside and allow to cool and thicken a little while making the pastry. Rub the margarine into the flour and salt, and bind with the egg. You should not require any liquid, but if too dry, add a teaspoon of milk. Divide the dough in two, and roll out each piece to about 9 inches square. Place one square on a greased baking sheet, spread with the fruit filling to within an inch from the edges, and put the other pastry piece on top. Seal the edges all round. Brush with beaten egg and prick with a fork. Bake for half an hour. Trim the edges, sprinkle with sugar and cut into squares.

Black piece

Ginger cake (adapted from Hotch Potch, *1951).*

8 oz plain flour	1 teasp ground ginger
2 oz butter or margarine	½ teasp bicarbonate of soda
2 oz caster sugar	1 egg
2 tablesp treacle	little warm water

Pre-heat oven to 180ºC/350ºF/gas mark 4. Grease a 7 inch square tin and dust with flour. Sift the dry ingredients and rub in the butter or margarine. Stir in the sugar. Beat the egg with the warmed treacle. Make a well in the dry ingredients, pour in the treacle mixture and beat together. Add warm water to soften the mixture. Place in the prepared tin. Bake for 30 minutes until brown.

Black bun

Dark and fruity, a Hogmanay speciality.

Pastry

12 oz plain flour	1 oz sugar
generous pinch salt	6 tablesp water
6 oz butter	

Filling

1 lb currants	1 teasp each of ground
1 lb raisins	ginger, cinnamon, allspice,
4 oz candied peel	nutmeg, cream of tartar,
8 oz chopped almonds	baking soda
8 oz plain flour	¼ pint whisky (optional)
8 oz soft brown sugar	little milk, egg yolk to glaze
2 eggs	

Pre-heat oven to 180ºC/350ºF/gas mark 4. Lightly grease an 8 inch round cake tin. Stir the flour with the sugar and salt, and rub in the butter. Bind to a stiff paste with the water. Roll out thinly and line the tin, keeping back a piece for the lid. In a large basin mix together all the filling ingredients by hand, adding just enough milk to moisten. Pack the mixture well into the pastry case. Flatten the top and lay on the lid, moistening the edges to seal. Prick all over the top with a fork and paint with the egg yolk to glaze. Bake for 3 hours. Cover the top with foil during the cooking to prevent over-browning, if necessary. Cool in the tin before turning out.

Sweeties

THE NORTHEASTER has always happily acknowledged his sweet tooth. He has a liking for the modest pandrop (mint imperial) which he probably first met in the kirk as a small child. This would be quietly passed to him by a watchful adult member of his family as the minister ascended the pulpit to deliver his sermon. With careful management, the pandrop could be made to last until the end of the minister's address.

Sweetie-making was a favourite evening pastime, especially in the winter, in pre-television days, and many people still enjoy making a tray of tablet. The Grampian sweetie eater is an expert on the finer points of that delicious titbit.

Butterscotch

An old favourite, smooth and mellow. The secret of making good butterscotch is to avoid stirring the mixture after the first melting stage.

1 lb granulated sugar	3 oz butter
good pinch of cream of tartar	vanilla essence or lemon juice

Put half a pint of water in a medium-size saucepan with a heavy base and dissolve the sugar in it over a low heat, stirring until every grain is gone. Take the pan from the heat to mix in the cream of tartar, then bring the mixture up to a gentle bubbling boil without stirring. After a few minutes, start testing for the 'soft ball' stage, when a little of the syrup dropped into a bowl of cold water will hold the shape of a soft ball when picked up. The mixture will reach this stage before it starts to darken in colour. Remove the pan from the heat and add the butter, already cut into thin slices. Use the point of a knife to push the butter into the hot mixture to help it melt quickly, but avoid stirring. Return to the heat and boil up gently for a few minutes. Again test a little of the mixture in cold water, this time for brittleness, the 'hard crack' stage. Sprinkle in a few drops of vanilla essence, or lemon juice if preferred (about half a lemon). Pour the toffee into an 8 inch oiled tin, but do not try to scrape down the mixture on the sides of the pan into the tin, as the sugar will grain out and spoil the toffee. Cool a little, then mark into butterscotch oblongs by pressing down evenly with a knife. When cold, break up and wrap the pieces.

Mealy candy

An old-fashioned farmhouse candy, dark and gingery.

1 lb granulated sugar	2 oz medium oatmeal
4 oz treacle	level dessertsp ground ginger

Spread the oatmeal in a small tin and toast under the grill until golden. Put the sugar, treacle and half pint of water in a medium-size heavy-base pan. Stir over a gentle heat until all the sugar is dissolved. Bring to the boil. Keep the mixture moving with a wooden spoon to prevent the treacle scorching. After boiling for 10 minutes remove from the heat, add the oatmeal and ginger, and beat until thick. Pour into a lightly-oiled 8 inch tin and mark into squares before completely cold.

White cream toffee

A special occasion sweet, rich and smooth. The modern UHT long-life creams, available in most supermarket cold cabinets, are reasonable in cost and have a good thick texture perfect for this recipe.

1 lb granulated sugar	½ pint carton (250 ml) UHT
4 oz butter	whipping cream

Put all the ingredients into a medium-size heavy-base saucepan and melt gently, until all the sugar is dissolved. Bring to the boil for 10 minutes and keep the toffee moving constantly with a wooden spoon to prevent sticking and to ensure that the mixture does not start to colour. Remove from the heat, tip the pan slightly and beat the toffee until thick. Pour into an oiled 8 inch tin. Mark into squares before cold.

Tablet

1½ lb granulated sugar
7 oz tin evaporated milk
   (unsweetened)
4 tablesp milk
½ teasp salt

4 oz butter (or a good
   margarine)
1 teasp treacle
vanilla essence

Put all the ingredients into a large heavy-base pan over the lowest setting on the cooker ring. Stir often until every grain of sugar has dissolved. Keep a pastry brush and bowl of warm water beside the pan. Every now and then, brush the sugary deposit from the sides of the pan down into the toffee. It will take about half an hour for all the sugar to dissolve. After this point, leave the toffee alone, with an occasional stir to keep it from catching on the pan bottom. It will gradually come to the boil even at this low temperature, and slowly darken. After half an hour, start testing for the soft ball, when a little of the mixture dropped into cold water holds its shape when picked up. When ready, remove the pan from the heat, stir in the vanilla essence and beat the toffee till thick, with an electric hand whisk if you have one as it is hard work. Pour into a 9 inch oiled tin and mark into squares or bars before completely set.

Note This is a good recipe to use if you are tied to the kitchen for some time, because it requires so little attention. At the low temperature used, there is no danger of the toffee boiling over the top of the pan.

Barley sugar

1 lb granulated sugar
good pinch cream of tartar

1 lemon
few sugar cubes (optional)

Rub a few sugar cubes, if you have some, over the lemon to absorb some of the essential oils in the skin. Put the cubes, sugar and half a pint of water in a medium-size saucepan with a heavy base. Heat gently and stir often until all the sugar has melted. Draw the pot from the heat and blend in the cream of tartar. Bring to the boil and stop stirring, to prevent the sugar from crystallising. When the syrup turns a golden amber, remove from the heat and sprinkle in the lemon juice, without stirring. As soon as the bubbles have died down, pour the mixture into an oiled swiss roll tin. Have ready a small bowl of oil, a spatula and a pair of kitchen scissors. Within a minute or two you should be able to lift up the candy at each end of the tin with the tip of the oiled spatula. Fold the ends of the toffee sides to middle, like a sheet, and cut it in two with the oiled scissors. Cut each half of the candy into strips, and twist each piece into the usual barley sugar shape. Keep your hands and tools oiled to make the work easy and quick, as the toffee hardens very soon.

Heather honey toffee

A 'pulled' candy. A recipe from Deeside.

2 cups sugar
¼ cup of cream
¼ cup of boiling water

3 rounded dessertsp heather
honey

Melt all the ingredients in a pan. Make sure all the sugar is dissolved. Bring slowly to the boil, stirring, then boil for 5 minutes without stirring. Drop a little in cold water, testing until it is brittle and has a good amber colour. Pour the mixture on to a cool, well-oiled, non-porous surface — ideally, a large marble slab, but a large flat dish will do. In a minute or two, when it begins to cool, start to go round the edges of the candy with the tip of a buttered spatula, lifting the toffee from the slab. Turn the outer edges sides to middle, like a sheet. When cool enough to handle, oil your hands lightly, gather up the candy and pull it out into a rope. Put the two ends back in one hand and pull out again. Pull and twist the rope until it is elastic and shiny and lighter in colour. Finally, cut the rope into small pieces with oiled scissors, twisting as you cut, to give the sweets a nice shape. Cool and store in a tin.

Black man

Traditional farmhouse toffee, popular fifty years ago, and made at that time from the molasses kept on the farms for mixing in the cattle mash. This recipe uses treacle which has a mellower flavour, and the quantities have been scaled down for family use, but it is made in exactly the same way.

1 lb treacle
1 teasp vinegar
pinch bicarbonate of soda

few drops of lemon, almond
or peppermint essence

Put the treacle and vinegar in a medium-size heavy-base pan. Bring gently to the boil, stirring to prevent the treacle scorching. This is important, to avoid a bitter flavour. Boil carefully for 10 minutes, then start testing it for set; it is ready when a little of the mixture will snap when dropped into cold water. Add your preferred flavouring and stir in the soda very thoroughly. Pour on to the cold oiled slab, turn sides to middle when cool enough, then 'pull' with oiled hands as described in previous recipe. Cut and wrap the sweets in waxed paper, as they are moist and chewy in texture. Traditionally, the sweet was cut into bars about 5 inches long.

Russian toffee

A chewy favourite from childhood days.

2 oz butter
4 oz caster sugar
1 rounded tablesp redcurrant
  jelly

2 level tablesp syrup
large can (approx 14 oz)
  sweetened condensed milk
1 teasp vanilla essence

Put the butter, syrup and sugar into a heavy-base pan and melt gently until the sugar is dissolved. Add the condensed milk and redcurrant jelly. At this point put a trivet or rack — I use a small wire cake cooling tray — under the pan, as this mixture burns easily on direct heat. Bring up to the boil, stirring constantly and occasionally moving the pot aside from the heat. The toffee takes only a few minutes to cook, and is ready when a teaspoonful dropped into a bowl of cold water forms a chewy ball. Stir in the vanilla essence and pour toffee into an oiled 7 inch tin, base-lined with non-stick baking parchment. Mark into squares when just warm. When cold, tip out of tin and cut into squares with kitchen scissors.

Swiss milk tablet

A favourite with children, and a popular sweet to make for sales of work and coffee mornings.

2 lb granulated sugar
4 oz butter or margarine
large tin sweetened
  condensed milk

½ cup of water
½ cup of milk
1 teasp vanilla essence

Put the sugar, butter, water and milk in a large heavy-base pan over a low heat. Stir until all the sugar grains have been dissolved, then bring gradually up to the boil and boil for 10 minutes without stirring. Stir in the condensed milk then boil for another 10 minutes. Remove from the heat and add the vanilla essence. Stir until the toffee begins to grain (for a better texture beat for 1 minute) then pour into a buttered tin. Mark into squares before completely cold.

Whisky truffles

Make these at Christmas, or for a party sweetmeat. For adults only, bittersweet and a little boozy. Substitute sherry for whisky if you prefer it.

12 oz shortcake biscuits
3 oz butter
3 oz icing sugar
3 level tablesp cocoa powder
1 level tablesp instant coffee
  granules

2 tablesp whisky
1 tablesp cream
vermicelli or cocoa powder
  for coating

Crush the biscuits finely in a food processor, or place them in a polythene bag and crush very thoroughly with a rolling pin. Blend the butter with the icing sugar. Dissolve the coffee granules in the whisky and cream. Work all the ingredients together in a bowl or in the processor. Form into balls about the size of a walnut and roll in cocoa powder or vermicelli to coat. Place in small paper sweet cases.

Turkish delight

It is worth using rose water — or orange flower water — for the lovely taste and aroma they give this delicate sweet. They are not expensive, and you can find them at the larger chemists or a delicatessen.

1 lb granulated sugar	1 tablesp lemon juice
½ pint water	few drops of pink food colour
1 oz powdered gelatine	2 tablesp icing sugar
1 tablesp rose water	1 tablesp cornflour

Stir the gelatine and the sugar together to mix evenly, then put in a medium-size, heavy-base pan with the water. Melt over a gentle heat until the solution is clear. Bring up to the boil and cook for 5 minutes, stirring lightly. Remove from the heat and stir in the lemon juice, rose water and one or two drops of colouring. Allow to cool for a minute or two, then draw a piece of kitchen paper across the surface to clear the mixture. Pour into a 6 inch oiled tin and leave to set overnight. Next day, mix the icing sugar and cornflour together, sprinkle the work surface and dust a sharp knife. Carefully ease the set mixture out of the tin. Cut into 6 strips, then cut each strip into 6 cubes. Toss each cube in the sugar and cornflour coating. Store in an airtight box, sprinkling the coating between each layer.

If serving as a table sweetmeat, arrange on a round tray with a tube of cocktail sticks in the middle.

Pantry

IN THE PAST, a well-stocked pantry was a priority of the northeast housewife, for reasons of economy as well as being a source of pride in her cooking skills. She was an expert jam and jelly maker, the provider of the familiar and well-loved 'jeely piece', the bread-and-jam tummy-filler which in lean years was much more than just a 'fine piece' between meals. In many families the jelly piece was main source of daily nourishment. Wild fruits grew in profusion all over Grampian — brambles, raspberries, rosehips, rowan berries — there for the picking, and they were taken eagerly to be preserved in jams, jellies, pickles, fruit vinegars and wines.

Tart-sweet Scottish raspberries are famed for their rich flavour, ripening slowly in the cool northern summer. Soft fruits grow extremely well in North-east gardens — the well-loved grossets (gooseberries), strawberries, red, white and black currants, and the old favourite rhubarb. In the spring you will see up-ended old bottomless buckets set over clumps of rhubarb, as their owners eagerly await the first tender pink stalks shooting up to the light.

More people are growing the cultivated thornless brambles, as hedgerows and copses give way to building developments, although it is still possible to find wild fruits quite easily. In September copses of elderberries are black with ripe fruits, great

70

umbrella heads of them. Set up in September, an elderberry wine will be ready, rich, ruby-red and port-like for Christmas of the following year.

In the late autumn, at the Great Garden of Pitmedden just north of Aberdeen, the air is heavy with the scent of ripening fan-trained apples and pears in a profusion of named varieties, along the high old walls. Some stone fruits do quite well in Grampian. In my own garden, a Victoria plum tree ripens to a honeyed sweetness.

I have a happy memory of childhood picnic/fruit picking outings, setting off with my parents in our high old black Ford, my father in flat cap and leather gloves, trundling along the sunny lanes at a daring 35 miles an hour. On the moors around Dinnet we found blaeberries and cranberries, and hedgerows thick with raspberries at Ardoe and south of Banchory. They are still there for the Grampian fruitpicker to find.

A few hints

An excellent substitute for muslin, for holding spices, is a piece of fine-mesh terylene window screening. Save the best pieces, when making up window screens, or when discarding old ones. They can safely be boiled to sterilise. Large pieces can be used to strain fruit in wine making.

When making pickles, jam jars are not very suitable for potting, as it is difficult to make them airtight with cellophane covers, and air reaching a pickle in storage will spoil it. Use a preserving skin such as Porosan. Screw-top jars such as coffee jars are best, but cover the mouth of the jar with a double piece of polythene to separate vinegar from metal, before screwing down the lid, or cover the pickle with ceresin paper (from large chemists).

To prepare jars for potting, wash thoroughly, dry and place in the oven at a low heat. They will become dry and very hot, and will not crack if a hot jam is poured in.

To test for a set, put a little of the preserve in a saucer to cool. Take the pan away from the heat while waiting, as it is possible for a preserve to go past the setting point. If ready, it will wrinkle when you push it with a finger. If not, return the pan to the heat and test again every 5 minutes.

JAMS

Rhubarb and ginger jam

3 lb rhubarb	2 lb sugar
1 large cooking apple	2 lemons
2 oz root ginger	2 oz crystallised ginger

Wash the rhubarb and cut into small chunks. Peel, core and chop the apple. Squeeze the juice from the lemons. Put the rhubarb, apple, sugar and lemon juice in a bowl overnight. Next day, transfer to a jelly pan. Bruise the ginger and tie in a muslin or terylene net bag with the lemon pips. Push it into the fruit. Add the sugar and melt over a low heat before bringing up to the boil. Boil the jam briskly for 10-15 minutes, then start testing for a set. When ready, remove the ginger bag, stir in the chopped crystallised ginger, and pot the jam in hot, sterilised jars.

Rhubarb and rose petal jam

1 lb rhubarb	1 lb sugar
juice of 1 lemon	4 oz red or pink rose petals

Wash and chop the rhubarb. Put the sugar, rhubarb and lemon juice in a bowl overnight. Next day, cut up the rose petals. Nip off the little white part at the base and discard. Add the petals to the fruit. Bring slowly to the boil, ensuring that the sugar is dissolved. Boil to setting point. Pour into small sterilised jars and cover.

Rose petal jam

This delicate, old-fashioned preserve is delicious in cream scones, or used as a topping for vanilla or strawberry ice cream. The petals can be taken from full-blown roses a little past their best, but make sure the flowers are dry when picked. Old-fashioned and species roses are best because of their rich scent. If taking petals from modern hybrid teas and floribundas, use only those with a strong scent.

1 pint rose petals	2 tablesp lemon juice
1 lb sugar	¼ pint water

Bring the water, sugar and lemon juice slowly to the boil, stirring to dissolve the sugar grains. Reduce heat to a simmer. Nip off the white part at the base of the petals as it is bitter, and add the petals to the syrup. Cook over the lowest possible heat, stirring all the time, for half an hour. The petals will turn clear. At this point, tint with one drop of red food colouring, if wished. Pot into small hot jars.

Greengage jam

Not expensive to make, but a luxury rarely seen in the shops.

3 lb greengages	3 lb sugar

Wash the fruit and poach gently in ½ pint water until the skins are tender. Add the sugar only when this stage has been reached. Stir until dissolved. Bring to the boil, and boil rapidly until the setting point is reached. Skim off the stones. Pour into hot clean jars. Cover.

Spiced bramble jam

6 lb brambles
2 lb demerara sugar
1 pint cider vinegar

1 teasp each ground ginger
and ground cinnamon

Bring the vinegar, sugar and spices slowly to the boil, stirring to dissolve the sugar grains. Add the cleaned brambles and simmer for 20 minutes. Test for a set. Pot into hot jars.

Note   Malt vinegar is not suitable for this recipe as its flavour is too harsh.

Blackcurrant jam

2 lb blackcurrants
juice and finely grated rind
of 1 lemon

5 lb sugar
water

This recipe yields 10 lb of jam. I wash the berries and remove any stalks (tails) but do not top them, as I think this is an unnecessary chore.
Put the berries into a preserving pan and, using a 1 lb jam jar as a measure, add 5 jars of water to the pan. Stir in the juice and rind. Bring up to the boil and cook for 10 minutes. Remove from the heat, add the sugar and stir to dissolve. Bring back to the boil and cook for 20 minutes. Pot into hot jars. The lemon adds a pleasant extra tartness to the jam.

Ginger marrow jam

4 lb prepared vegetable
    marrow
4 lb sugar

2 lemons
2 oz root ginger, or 4 level
    teasp ground ginger

Peel the marrow and cut into ½ inch dice, to obtain 4 lb weight. Grate the rind from the lemons, avoiding the pith, and stir into the diced marrow. Cover with the sugar and allow to stand for 24 hours. Put the mixture into a preserving pan and add the lemon juice with either the powdered ginger or root ginger bruised and tied into a piece of muslin or terylene netting. Bring slowly to the boil, stirring all the time to dissolve the sugar. Reduce the heat and simmer for half an hour, until the marrow is tender and has turned clear. Discard the bag of ginger, if using, and test for a set. If not ready, boil up and test again after a few minutes. It may be necessary to add a little water to the marrow to prevent it sticking. When ready, pot into hot jars.

Apricot and ginger preserve

A small treat.

½ lb fresh apricots
2 tablesp lemon juice
½ lb granulated sugar

2 pieces preserved stem
ginger (about 2 oz) or 2 oz
crystallised ginger

Stone and chop the apricots. Crack the stones and remove the kernels. Put the fruit, kernels, lemon juice and finely chopped ginger into a pan. Bring slowly to the boil, stirring to dissolve the sugar. Cook gently so as not to break up the fruit, until the syrup is setting. Pour into hot sterilised small jars, including some of the kernels for flavour, and seal in the usual way.

Freezer jam

Uncooked jam with a fresh sharp flavour.

2½-3 lb fruit
1 lemon

4 lb sugar
bottle liquid pectin

Put the fruit, crushed or sliced as appropriate, into a bowl with the sugar and juice squeezed from the lemon. Mix well and leave in a warm place for a few hours. Stir occasionally so that all the sugar dissolves. Add the bottle of liquid pectin. Stir for 2 minutes so that it is thoroughly mixed in. Leave 24 hours to mature, then ladle into small containers. Freeze. Thaw for 2 hours before using, and store in the fridge. Use from the freezer within 6 months.

JELLIES

General method for making a fruit jelly

Cover the fruit with cold water, bring to the boil, and simmer until tender. Strain the fruit and liquid overnight through muslin, fine netting or a proprietary jelly bag, into a large bowl. The easiest way to do this is to tie the bag to the legs of an up-ended stool or chair. Do not squeeze the bag or the jelly will be cloudy. Measure the juice obtained into a preserving pan. For each pint of juice, add 1 tablespoon lemon juice. Some cooks like to add 2 cloves for each pint of juice. Allow 1 lb sugar for each pint, and heat slowly, stirring until the grains are dissolved. Boil gently to set — this usually takes about 15-20 minutes. Pot and cover.

This method can be used for any fruit.

Raspberry and blackcurrant jelly

Using the general method, an especially delicious jelly can be made using 2 lb of raspberries mixed with 2 lb of blackcurrants. Use as a sauce for ice cream or a filling, with whipped cream or dessert topping, for the sponge sandwich on page 60.

Redcurrant jelly

For an especially fruity redcurrant jelly, use only a small amount of water.

Put the redcurrants into a preserving pan with about ¼ pint of water. Bring to the boil and simmer until the fruit is pulped. Allow to drip through a jelly bag overnight. Continue as for the general method.

Bramble jelly

An alternative method for bramble jelly, using only fruit and sugar.

Pre-heat oven to 180°C/350°F/gas mark 4. Spread the berries out on baking trays and bake until they are soft. Put the fruit into a jelly bag and allow to drip overnight. Do not squeeze the bag. Measure the juice and add 1 lb of sugar for each pint. Bring slowly up to the boil, stirring, and cook briskly until the liquid gels. Pot into hot jars.

Some fruit jellies are very suitable for use as accompaniments to meat and game.

Rowan jelly

Make as for general method. Crush the berries with a wooden spoon as they cook, to extract all the juice. When boiling up the juice and sugar mixture, it may be half an hour before you obtain a set for the jelly. Two apples chopped into the berries without peeling or coring are helpful in encouraging a set more quickly.

Apple and bramble port jelly

A special jelly to accompany Christmas meats.

Simmer 2 lb cooking apples and 2 lb brambles in 1½ pints water and ½ pint port. Crush the fruit with a wooden spoon as it cooks. Strain through a jelly bag overnight. If there is more than 3 pints of juice, boil to reduce. Add 3 lb sugar and proceed as for the general method.

MARMALADES

Whisky marmalade

1½ lb Seville oranges
2 sweet oranges
2 lemons

3 lb granulated sugar
4 tablesp whisky

Shred the peel finely, avoiding the pith. Squeeze out the juice. Put the peel into a pan with a muslin or terylene net bag containing the pips, pith and tissues from the fruit, and 4 pints of water. Bring to the boil, reduce heat and simmer for 1½ hours, to reduce the liquid to no more than 3 pints. Draw the pan from the heat, discard the muslin bag and stir in the sugar until completely dissolved. Boil rapidly until setting point is reached. This can take from 20 minutes to 45 minutes according to the type of pan used — in an ordinary large saucepan it will take longer than in a preserving pan. Stir in whisky just before potting.

YIELDS 5 lb

Three-fruit marmalade

A small quantity (about 3 lb) quickly made with the help of a mincer.

1 orange
1 lemon

1 grapefruit
2 lb sugar

Wash fruit, halve and squeeze out the juice. With a spoon, scrape out the pith and pips and tie these in a piece of muslin or terylene net. Put the peel through the mincer and into a large saucepan (8 pints). Add 1 pint of water, bring to the boil and simmer 30 minutes or until the peel is tender. Remove from the heat. Discard the bag of pips. Add the sugar and stir until completely dissolved. Bring to the boil and cook until setting point is reached — start testing for a set after about 15 minutes. Pot and cover.

Lemon and pineapple marmalade

A winter favourite from store-cupboard ingredients, when we are running low on marmalade before the new season. Makes 5 to 6 lb.

1 lb 14 oz can Mamade
  prepared lemons for
  marmalade

1 lb can pineapple rings in
  own juice
3¾ lb sugar

Put the lemon concentrate and sugar into a jelly pan over a low heat. Add the pineapple, chopped into half-inch wedges, and the juice, made up to one pint with cold water. Stir till the sugar is dissolved, then bring up to the boil for about 15 minutes. Test for set. When ready, pot into hot jars. Allow to cool completely before covering.

FRUIT CURDS, CHEESES AND BUTTERS

Fruit curds *are made mostly from citrus fruits, and some very sharp fruits such as gooseberry. Make in small quantities to enjoy fresh. As they contain eggs and butter, home-made curds should be used up within a month or two. Store in a cool larder. Once opened keep them in the fridge.*

Fruit cheeses *were made as an alternative to the cheese course, thick sweetened purees, often spiced, set in small shaped moulds. Eat with plain breads, scones or biscuits. They also go well with meats — and cheese.*

Fruit butters *are a softer version of fruit cheese, and spread easily. They have a sharper flavour than jams.*

Lemon curd

2 large lemons	3 oz butter
8 oz sugar	2 eggs

Grate rind lightly from lemons, avoiding the pith. Squeeze out the juice. Put lemon rind, juice, sugar and butter in a bowl set over a pan of boiling water. Cook until the butter is melted and the sugar completely dissolved. Take the bowl from the heat. Beat the eggs together, then stir into the butter mixture. From this point, keep the water at a low simmer, and stir the mixture for about 10 minutes till it thickens enough to coat the back of a spoon. Do not let it boil or it will curdle. Pour into clean warmed pots and cover like jam. The curd will thicken in the pot. For a sharper-tasting curd, use 7 oz of sugar.

St Clement's curd
As for lemon curd, using one orange and one lemon.

Lime curd
As for lemon curd, but use 4 limes and an additional ounce of sugar.

Gooseberry curd

1 lb hard green gooseberries	2 oz butter
6 oz sugar	2 eggs

Wash, top and tail the gooseberries. Cook gently with 2 tablespoons water for 20 minutes until tender. If possible, liquidise the fruit then sieve to remove the seeds. This makes an especially rich and thick curd. Otherwise, push the fruit through a sieve. Put the puree in a bowl with the sugar and butter, and continue as for lemon curd. A little less sugar may be used for a sharper taste.

The addition of half a teaspoon of ground ginger to the curd gives an interesting difference to the flavour.

Apple cheese

3 lb cooking apples
¾ pint dry cider

1 level teasp ground allspice
sugar

Quarter the apples and cut out the core. Chop up the fruit without peeling. Cook in a saucepan with the cider for about 10 minutes, until pulpy. Push the apples through a sieve. Measure the pulp and allow 12 oz sugar to each pint of pulp. Return to the rinsed pan, add the allspice and heat gently to melt the sugar. Boil fairly rapidly until the pulp thickens and a wooden spoon drawn across the pan base leaves a clean line. This can take up to an hour. Stir frequently. If to be used soon, pour into little moulds moistened with glycerine, or pot into small clean sterilised jars. Serve with bread and butter or in tarts.

Plum butter

2 lb ripe plums
1 pint cider or apple juice

1 level teasp cinnamon
sugar

Wash and chop the fruit, and discard the stones. Simmer in the cider or juice until soft. Push through a sieve. Allow 12 oz sugar to every 1 lb of puree. Melt slowly with the cinnamon in a pan, until the sugar is dissolved. Boil fairly rapidly until the mixture is thick and the liquid has been driven off, but is still of a spreading consistency. Pot into small sterilised jars.

VINEGAR PRESERVES

Both vegetables and fruit can be preserved in spiced vinegar. Vegetables are usually soaked in brine before pickling, to draw off water which would weaken the vinegar so that the pickle will not keep.

Good-quality pickling spice can be bought ready-mixed and can save the expense of buying a range of spices you may not otherwise use. (Incidentally, for a person cooking on a modest scale, a jar of pickling spice can provide a small store of spices to pick out for use in a whole range of recipes.) Use 1 oz of pickling spice to 1 pint of vinegar.

Spiced vinegar

If you prefer to make up your own spice mix, this is a basic recipe.

2 pints malt vinegar
1 stick cinnamon
few peppercorns

1 level tablesp each of cloves,
mace, whole allspice

If you prefer a 'hotter' taste, add
1 tablesp each of mustard seed and whole crushed chillies

(a) The best result is obtained by soaking the spices, tied in a muslin bag, in the cold vinegar, for about 2 months. Occasionally open the jar, to stir. Lay a polythene bag across the mouth of the jar before screwing on the lid, to avoid contact between the vinegar and the metal lid.

(b) *Quick method* Heat the ingredients together in an uncovered saucepan until boiling. Pour into a bowl, cover and leave for 3 hours. Strain. Store in bottles and seal, if not using immediately.

PICKLED VEGETABLES

Beetroot

Wash the beets but do not peel. Simmer in salted water for 1½ hours. Allow to cool in the water. Peel and slice, or leave small ones whole. Pack into sterilised jars and cover with the cold spiced vinegar. Seal with vinegar-proof lids.

Nasturtium seeds

(Mock capers.) An old cottage pickle.

Pick the seeds when plump and fully ripe at the end of the season. Rinse the seeds and soak in a brine of 2 oz coarse household salt dissolved in 1 pint of water for 24 hours. Put an upturned plate into the brine on top of the seeds to keep them submerged. Drain and pack into small sterilised jars. Cover with the cold spiced vinegar, and seal. Keep 1 month before using. Use in fish dishes.

Note Table salt must not be used, as it contains chemicals to make it free-flowing, but which will taint the pickle.

PICKLED FRUITS

Sugar is added to a spiced vinegar for fruits.

Pickled plums

Serve with cold meats — especially good with pork. The addition of the gently aromatic blackcurrant leaves is an old-fashioned touch. Their use is optional.

3 lb ripe firm plums	1 level teasp salt
1 oz pickling spice	1 lb demerara sugar
thinly pared rind of small	1 pint vinegar
lemon	blackcurrant leaves (optional)

Wash the plums and prick with darning needle. Put the vinegar into a saucepan with the spice, lemon rind, salt and sugar. Heat gently, stirring to dissolve the sugar. Add the plums and simmer until just tender. The fruit should not break up. Lift them out gently and pack in hot dry jars, with a blackcurrant leaf on the bottom, in the middle, and on the top of the plums, if liked. Boil the vinegar mixture until reduced and slightly syrupy. Pour over the fruit to cover completely. Allow to cool, then screw on vinegar-proof lids, or line with polythene. Allow to mature at least 2 months.

Spiced prunes

Eat with cold or hot meats.

1 lb prunes	grated rind 1 lemon
2 pints cold tea, strained	¾ pint vinegar
1 teasp pickling spice	½ lb granulated sugar
10 cloves	

Soak the prunes in the tea overnight. Next day, cook the prunes in the tea until plump but still firm, about 10-15 minutes. Drain, reserving the liquid. Put the vinegar, sugar and cloves in a pan. Bring slowly to the boil, stirring to dissolve the sugar, then simmer gently for 10 minutes. Add half a pint of the reserved tea liquid and bring to the boil. Boil for 10 minutes to reduce the liquid until slightly syrupy. Pour over the prunes, adding the cloves to the jars. Cover and seal. They are ready to eat within a week.

Pickled brambles

A tasty recipe with all roast meats or cold cuts. Cider vinegar is best for the recipe, but malt vinegar will do.

2½ lb brambles

Spiced vinegar

1 pint cider vinegar	1 level teasp each, ground
1 lb soft brown sugar	nutmeg, ground ginger,
1 stick cinnamon	ground allspice
1 bay leaf	

Put the cider vinegar and spices in a pan and bring to the boil. Simmer for 5 minutes, then cover and set aside overnight to infuse. Next day, strain the vinegar and dissolve the brown sugar in it over a gentle heat. Add the brambles and cook gently for 5 minutes. Remove the berries with a slotted spoon and pack into clean hot jars. Boil the liquid in the pan for 5 minutes until reduced and syrupy. Pour over the brambles. Seal. Allow to mature for 1 month before opening.

FRUIT VINEGARS

Fruit vinegars were used in grandmother's day mostly as a soothing remedy for sore throats. Modern cooks are finding other uses for them — for toppings, for drinks and salad dressings, to name a few. Broken or less than perfect fruit can be used, but discard any showing traces of mould.

Raspberry vinegar

1 lb raspberries	1 pint malt or white wine
sugar	vinegar

Crush the raspberries in a bowl and add the vinegar. Cover and leave for 1 week, stirring every day. Strain liquid through kitchen paper in a nylon sieve and allow 1 lb of sugar to every pint of liquid. Dissolve sugar and boil for 10 minutes. Pour into hot dry bottles and seal.

Bramble vinegar

Make in the same way. For extra flavour, add a broken cinnamon stick and the finely grated peel of a small orange (no pith) to the bowl for the week while it is steeping.

Suggestions for use

 For a refreshing summer drink, try a fruit vinegar topped up with soda water.

 They can be used as a fruity topping for a plain milk pudding.

 When having ice cream in a dish or a cappie (cone) at home, revive the old custom of putting a shake of raspberry vinegar on the top of the ice cream. As a child, I thought this the best part of a cappie.

CHUTNEYS

Beetroot chutney

3 lb beetroot	½ teasp salt
2 lb apples	1 teasp ground ginger
2 onions	2 lb sugar
1 pint vinegar	1 lemon

Wash the beetroot, and boil unpeeled for 1½ hours. Allow to cool in the water, then peel them and cut into small cubes. Peel and chop the apples and onions. Squeeze the juice from the lemon. Put the apples and onions into a pan with the vinegar, lemon juice, sugar, salt and ginger. Boil for 20 minutes. Add the beetroot cubes and cook for another 20 minutes. Allow to cool, then pot into sterilised jars. Keep for two weeks before opening.

Apricot chutney

Especially delicious with a curry.

3 lb apricots
1 lb cooking apples
2 large onions, finely chopped
6 cloves garlic, chopped fine
1 oz green ginger, peeled and
   chopped fine

½ pint malt vinegar
1 level teasp salt
12 oz soft brown sugar
½ teasp ground chilli (more
   if liked)

Tie in a muslin bag
piece of cinnamon stick
6 cloves

12 peppercorns

Wash, halve and stone the apricots but do not peel. Peel and slice the apples. Crack the apricot stones to obtain the kernels. Put everything in a large pan, including the apricot kernels. Simmer gently until the fruit is soft and all the sugar dissolved. Bring to a fast boil for 10 minutes to thicken. Remove the spice bag, squeezing it to extract the flavourings. Discard the apricot kernels. Pot into sterilised jars when cool. It is not important for a chutney to have a firm set.

CITRUS

Spiced lemons in oil

These preserved lemons are very useful to the cook. Put a whole drained lemon inside a chicken before roasting, for flavour and moistness. Sliced lemon can be added to meat and chicken casseroles as a tenderiser, and for flavour. Use the oil for cooking purposes, for salad dressings and mayonnaise. A large sweet jar with a glass stopper is very suitable, as well as attractive, as an airtight seal is not necessary.

lemons
cloves

corn, sunflower or olive oil

Wash some thin-skinned lemons and stud with cloves. Pack into a large glass jar and pour in the oil to cover. Cover and leave for a month before starting to use.

Candied peel

A tangy Christmas titbit.

orange, lemon and grapefruit
   peel, from 6 pieces of fruit
½ teasp bicarbonate of soda

1 lb granulated sugar
caster sugar

Cut the peel into strips ¼ inch wide, and 1½-2 inches long. Soak the peel for 15 minutes in a pint of boiling water with bicarbonate of soda dissolved in it. Drain and rinse. Cover with cold water, bring to the boil and simmer for 20 minutes or until tender — lemon peel can take a little longer. Drain and rinse. Dissolve sugar in ½ pint of water, making sure all the grains have gone. Bring up to the boil, add the peel and simmer 40 minutes to 1 hour, until the peel has absorbed most of the syrup and has turned glossy and transparent. Remove the peel with a slotted spoon, letting the excess syrup drop off. Roll in caster sugar. Place a wire cooling rack on a baking sheet and arrange the peel on top so that the pieces do not touch each other. Dry out in a cool oven — the lowest setting — for at least an hour with the door a little open. Roll the strips in more caster sugar after drying. Store in an airtight box between layers of greaseproof or waxed paper.

DECORATIONS

Chocolate leaves

2 oz chocolate (cooking
chocolate is suitable)

leaves

Choose shapely veined leaves such as privet or roses. Melt the chocolate on a small plate over a pan of hot water. With a knife, coat the *back* of the leaf with chocolate so that the chocolate will take the impression of the veins. Lay the leaves on a small tray and chill to harden. Carefully pull away the leaf and discard. Store the chocolate leaves in a box and use to decorate puddings and cakes.

Crystallised flowers

Crystallised rose petals and violets for decorating cakes are often seen, but other flowers and leaves are safe to eat, such as primroses, carnation petals, sweet peas, the pretty blue flowers of the herb borage, and mint leaves.

A short-term method only. They will keep for a few weeks.

1 egg white

caster sugar

Have two bowls ready, one with lightly beaten egg white, the other with caster sugar. If doing rose petals, nip off the little white part at the base, which is bitter. Gently paint the flower or petal with egg white using a child's paint brush. Let the excess egg white drop off. Sprinkle caster sugar over the flower or petal, to cover completely. Lay on greaseproof paper on a cake rack to dry off, in an airy place. Store in airtight jars between layers of greaseproof paper. Mint leaves can be crystallised in the same way.

WINES

Wines are simple to make. The only firm rule is the observation of strict cleanliness, of hands and equipment. Campden tablets, readily available at chemists, are useful for sterilising, and a crushed tablet added to the wine at bottling stage will help to preserve it.

Elderberry wine

A simple recipe for an inexpensive, full-bodied red wine.

3 lb elderberries	wine yeast, port type
3½ lb sugar	nutrient

Strip the berries from the stalks with the prong of a fork, then weigh. Rinse the fruit in a colander before crushing in a large sterilised container (I use a white plastic lidded bucket, kept only for wine-making). Pour on 1 gallon of boiling water. Allow to cool to lukewarm before adding the yeast and nutrient. Cover closely. Leave for 3 days, stirring daily. Strain through scalded muslin (or terylene net) on to the sugar. Stir to dissolve the sugar completely. Pour the liquid into a dark glass fermentation jar (to prevent the beautiful colour from fading — or tie a brown paper jacket round a clear jar) up to the shoulder, and plug with cotton-wool for a few days until the first fast fermentation is over. When quieter, use the reserved liquid to fill up to the neck and fit an airlock. Leave until the fermentation is complete — this can take a few months — then siphon the wine into another fermentation jar containing a crushed Campden tablet. Top up with cool boiled water, seal, and leave the wine to mature until required. Siphon into dark sterilised bottles shortly before intended use. If preferred, the wine can be bottled immediately after the addition of the Campden tablet, and stored until required.

Apple wine

'Chippit' (damaged) fruits are suitable for making wine.

6 lb apples	1 lemon
3 lb sugar	wine yeast (white)
½ lb chopped raisins	1 gallon water

Wash and cut up the apples. Boil with the raisins for 15 minutes in a gallon of water. Tip into a large clean container and stir in the sugar to dissolve. Allow to cool to lukewarm before adding the yeast activated according to the packet instructions. Cover the container closely and allow to ferment for 4 days, stirring once daily. Strain into a fermentation jar and fit an airlock. Leave until the fermentation is complete. Siphon and bottle as decribed for elderberry wine.

Bramble liqueur

A recipe from W. Davidson, Aberdeen. A delicious Christmas and New Year liqueur.

about 8 lb brambles
sugar

1 pint brandy

Put berries in a stone jar and then stand it in a saucepan of water and simmer until the juice is all out of the berries. Do not on any account allow the water to get into the jar. Strain through a jelly bag. Allow to get cold. Add 10 oz sugar (granulated) to each 1 pint of juice and boil for 4 minutes. When cold add 1 pint of brandy. Pour into empty spirit bottles. Cork and label.

Raspberry liqueur

8 oz raspberries
8 oz granulated sugar

¾ pint water
1 pint gin

Put the gin and fruit into a screw-top jar, screw down tightly and put into a warm spot, perhaps the airing cupboard, for a few days. Prepare a syrup by boiling the sugar and water together. Skim well. Strain the gin and fruit through a piece of scalded muslin or fine terylene netting, and add the cold syrup to the liquid. To clarify the liqueur, filter it through a jelly bag or a cone filter fitted with a coffee filter paper. Bottle and cork tightly.

Rumtopf

This is an easy but very special way of preserving fresh fruits as they come into season. Traditionally, a large earthenware crock is used, but a large glass sweetie jar with a plastic screw-top lid is suitable — give it a brown paper jacket to protect the fruit from the light. Any fruits can be used, although the skins of currants and gooseberries toughen a little in the rumtopf.

1 pint rum or brandy,
    cheapest brand
fresh fruits as they come into
    season

caster sugar

Put the rum or brandy into the crock. Add one cup of fruit, cleaned and prepared, and ½ cup caster sugar. Stir well, cover, and keep in a cool place, repeating the process as fruits become available, up to 12 cups. For larger rumtopfs, increase the ingredient proportions. When the last fruit has been added, cover the crock and leave it to mature. The initial harsh flavour will mellow, and a rumtopf started in early summer with the first strawberries will be ready for Christmas. As a suggestion, you might like to begin with quartered strawberries, followed by halved and stoned cherries, raspberries, sliced stoned apricots, sliced pineapple, peeled and sliced peaches, stoned and sliced plums, and perhaps ending with a few ripe brambles.

To serve Serve with ice cream, whipped cream, yogurt, or cream and yogurt mixed. The rumtopf juice, which is very sweet, makes a superb base syrup for a special fruit salad, especially at Christmas. Offer it as an alternative to Christmas pudding, using strawberries or raspberries from the freezer. Plums and red-skinned apples sliced into the juice are another happy combination for a fresh fruit salad.

Index